CELTIC TREASURE
Daily Scriptures and Prayer

CELTIC TREASURE

Daily Scriptures and Prayer

J. PHILIP NEWELL

William B. Eerdmans Publishing Company
Grand Rapids, Michigan

First published in 2005
in the U.K. by
The Canterbury Press Norwich
and in the United States of America by
Wm. B. Eerdmans Publishing Company
255 Jefferson Ave. S.E., Grand Rapids, Michigan 49503
www.eerdmans.com

Images in this book are from the Book of Kells,
reproduced by permission of Trinity College, Dublin/Bridgeman Art Library,
and from children's paintings based on the Book of Kells,
reproduced by permission of Carol Marples and the author

Typeset by Vera Brice
Printed and bound in Singapore

10 09 08 07 06 05   5 4 3 2 1

ISBN 0-8028-2983-X

To
Harry William MacPhail Cant
friend and father-in-law
preacher and pray-er
art-lover and wordsmith
Christian and Celt

CONTENTS

PREFACE

Celtic Treasure is an illuminated book of scripture and prayer for today. It is a fresh expression of an ancient tradition. In Celtic spirituality, as in so many of the world's great streams of religious devotion, prayer books and sacred scriptures have been beautifully illustrated over the centuries. The result is manuscripts that are not only beautiful to read and hear but also to see and handle. This is the aim of *Celtic Treasure*, as it was of two of my previous publications, *Celtic Benediction* and *Sounds of the Eternal*.

The difference with *Celtic Treasure* is that, as well as being a prayer book, it is a scripture book. There has always been a great love of scripture in the Celtic tradition. There is a delight in the Bible's central themes of creation and justice, wisdom and hope, vision and love. Seven of these themes give shape to the passages of scripture that I have rewritten for *Celtic Treasure*. Book One focuses on the theme of creation as an expression of the mystery of God. Book Two explores the theme of journey and promise in our lives. Book Three considers the tension between power and justice in the world. Book Four listens for the wisdom that God has placed deep within us. Book Five expresses the songs of joy and sadness that issue from the heart. Book Six looks at Christ as the face of God and the true face of the human soul. And Book Seven celebrates love as the greatest expression of our depths.

But why rewrite passages of scripture? I believe there is the need for a new simplicity and beauty of language for today. Fewer and fewer people in the western world are reading scripture, in part because of the sheer volume and density of the text. And fewer and fewer children are hearing it read at their family tables. *Celtic Treasure* is in no sense a replacement for actually reading the Bible itself. It is, however, an attempt to enable us, both as individuals and as families, to draw regularly from the great treasure-trove of scripture. After all, it is the primary text for our Christian spirituality, as well as one of the world's greatest literary inheritances.

Celtic Treasure can be used by individuals on their own. Its primary conception, however, is as a book that people will use together in their homes in the context of family life and relationship. I imagine it being used at the table: for instance, before or after an evening meal. It begins with the simple lighting of a candle and time for silence. It then retells a passage of scripture before moving towards prayer for the life of the world. Then it concludes with words of blessing that accompany the putting out of the candle light. But my hope is that readers will feel free to adapt its simple use and words to other times of the day and to other contexts and settings, whether outside or in churches or other gathering places.

Because I have aimed at beauty and simplicity of language, and because I envisage the book to be a resource for families, my principal workmate in the project has been Cameron, my nine-year-old son. As I rewrote passages of scripture I asked Cameron to read them aloud to me. If he stumbled or appeared not to understand what I had written, I knew that I needed to go back to the drawing board. This is not to say that everything in the book will be understood equally by young and old alike, but it is my hope that even a child will find enough here to stay engaged. For the very young its primary value lies in the simple act of gathering together as a family to light a candle, to hear a story and to say simple prayers for those in the world whom we know and love. This is not a children's book but I do hope that it has a childlike simplicity about it.

So my primary thanks are to Cameron for his vital editing role. I would also like to thank Christine Smith, my publisher, consistently a delight to work with, and whose idea it was to incorporate children's art into some of the design for the book. And there is Carol Marples, an Edinburgh artist friend, who skilfully enabled a group of fifteen children in Scotland to observe Celtic patterns of art in *The Book of Kells* and to reproduce these in their own paintings. The children were fun to work with and proved the point that poetic utterance and visual art belong together. And there is dear Jane Owen, who has supported budding artists over her long lifetime and saw the value of children participating in this project. Also there is Vera Brice, our London graphics artist, who in a number of projects now has beautifully woven together text and illumination. And finally there is my wife, Ali, who combines total support for me with uninhibited criticism of my writings. Both are essential to this work, which I hope will in a modest way further awaken us to the treasure that is in us all.

J. Philip Newell
Cathedral of The Isles
Cumbrae, Scotland

CELTIC TREASURE

BOOK ONE

Stories of Creation

DAY ONE
Opening Words
(as candle is lit)

We light a light
in the name of the God who creates life,
in the name of the Saviour who loves life,
in the name of the Spirit who is the fire of life.

*(Be still and aware of God's presence within
and all around)*

Scripture

In the beginning God created the heavens and the earth.
Before that there was only empty darkness and the deep
    eternal waters.
But in the dark a wind began to stir.
It was the breath of life.
It was God saying, 'Let there be light.'
And there was light.
God saw that it was good.
There was a time for light and a time for darkness.
The light was called day and the darkness night.
And there was evening and morning, creation's first day.

(from Genesis 1)

Let the nights and the days bless you, O God.
Let both light and dark bless you.
For you are the God of all creation.

(from Prayer of Azariah)

(A time for reflection on the reading – silent or spoken)

Prayer

In the silence of our hearts or in spoken words
let us give thanks for the gift of this day
and pray for the life of the world . . .

(Here brief prayers may be offered)

O God of light,
from whom all life flows,
may we glimpse the shinings of your presence in all things.
In the darknesses of our world,
in places of fear and terrible wrong,
and in the darknesses of our own lives,
in times of confusion and doubt,
may we glimpse the shinings of your life-giving presence.

Closing Words
(after which candle is extinguished)

The blessings of heaven,
the blessings of earth,
the blessings of sea and of sky.
On those we love this day
and on every human family
the gifts of heaven,
the gifts of earth,
the gifts of sea and of sky.

DAY TWO

Opening Words
(as candle is lit)

We light a light
in the name of the God who creates life,
in the name of the Saviour who loves life,
in the name of the Spirit who is the fire of life.

*(Be still and aware of God's presence within
and all around)*

Scripture

On the second day the storm kept stirring.
It was the wind of new beginnings.
God was saying, 'Let there be a space for creation.'
And the wind carved out a hollow in the deep waters.
It was a cradle for life.
Above, beneath and on every side of it were the everlasting waters.
God saw that it was good.
It was a place for birth and abundance.
And there was evening and morning, creation's second day.

(from Genesis 1)

Blessed are you in the heights and the depths, O God.
Let the eternal waters praise you.
Let the winds and all that stirs life into motion praise you.
For you are the God of all creation.

(from Prayer of Azariah)

(A time for reflection on the reading – silent or spoken)

Prayer

In the silence of our hearts or in spoken words
let us give thanks for the gift of this day
and pray for the life of the world . . .

(Here brief prayers may be offered)

O God of life,
who chooses creation over chaos
and new beginnings over emptiness,
we bring to you the disorder of our nations and world
and the emptiness of our lives and relationships.
Bless us and the nations with the grace of creativity.
Bless us and all people with the hope of new beginnings.

Closing Words
(after which candle is extinguished)

The blessings of heaven,
the blessings of earth,
the blessings of sea and of sky.
On those we love this day
and on every human family
the gifts of heaven,
the gifts of earth,
the gifts of sea and of sky.

DAY THREE
Opening Words
(as candle is lit)

We light a light
in the name of the God who creates life,
in the name of the Saviour who loves life,
in the name of the Spirit who is the fire of life.

*(Be still and aware of God's presence within
and all around)*

Scripture

On the third day God said, 'Let the firm earth appear.'
So the wind gathered together the waters of life.
The waters were oceans and the dry land was earth.
The wind blew over its dark soil.
Earth grew green.
Flowers in their freshness opened.
Colour and goodness burst forth from the earth.
Young bushes budded.
Trees were heavy with fruit and earth's seed was strong.
God saw that it was good.
And there was evening and morning, creation's third day.

(from Genesis 1)

Let the mountains and hills, the fields and valleys bless you, O God.
Let all that is green and grows from the ground bless you.
For you are the God of all creation.

(from Prayer of Azariah)

(A time for reflection on the reading – silent or spoken)

Prayer

In the silence of our hearts or in spoken words
let us give thanks for the gift of this day
and pray for the life of the world . . .

(Here brief prayers may be offered)

The earth is full of your goodness, O God.
It sprouts green and grows into the roundness of fruit.
Its touch and its taste enliven our souls.
Let us know the seeds of life's goodness within us and between us.
And let us handle its gifts with wonder.

Closing Words
(after which candle is extinguished)

The blessings of heaven,
the blessings of earth,
the blessings of sea and of sky.
On those we love this day
and on every human family
the gifts of heaven,
the gifts of earth,
the gifts of sea and of sky.

DAY FOUR

Opening Words
(as candle is lit)

We light a light
in the name of the God who creates life,
in the name of the Saviour who loves life,
in the name of the Spirit who is the fire of life.

*(Be still and aware of God's presence within
and all around)*

Scripture

On the fourth day God said, 'Let there be lights in the heavens.'
So the wind carried fire on its wings and scattered light through
   the skies.
There was a great light to rule the day and a gentler light
   to rule the night.
And there were glittering galaxies beyond number.
The sun, the moon and the stars moved in harmony.
They guided the seasons.
They marked the days and the years.
They shone on earth as signs of heaven.
God saw that it was good.
And there was evening and morning, creation's fourth day.

                                        (from Genesis 1)

Blessed are you in the high heavens, O God.
Let the sun and the moon praise you.
Let the stars and all that shines with glory praise you.
For you are the God of all creation.

                           (from Prayer of Azariah)

(A time for reflection on the reading – silent or spoken)

Prayer

In the silence of our hearts or in spoken words
let us give thanks for the gift of this day
and pray for the life of the world . . .

(Here brief prayers may be offered)

In the rising of the sun and its setting,
in the whiteness of the moon and its seasons,
in the infinity of space and its shining stars
you are God and we bless you.
May we know the harmony of heaven in the relationships of earth
and may we know the expanse of its mystery within us.

Closing Words

(after which candle is extinguished)

The blessings of heaven,
the blessings of earth,
the blessings of sea and of sky.
On those we love this day
and on every human family
the gifts of heaven,
the gifts of earth,
the gifts of sea and of sky.

DAY FIVE
Opening Words
(as candle is lit)

We light a light
in the name of the God who creates life,
in the name of the Saviour who loves life,
in the name of the Spirit who is the fire of life.

*(Be still and aware of God's presence within
and all around)*

Scripture

On the fifth day God said, 'Let the waters bring forth living creatures.'
So the wind awakened the waters into life.
Great sea-monsters were born.
Gleaming fish swarmed the seas.
Winged birds of every kind rose out of the waters.
Creeping things crawled from the sea.
Wild animals ran free.
And cattle roamed the grasslands.
God saw that it was good.
Earth was alive with its creatures.
And there was evening and morning, creation's fifth day.

(from Genesis 1)

Blessed are you in earth, sea and sky, O God.
Let the whales and everything that swims praise you.
Let the birds and all creatures of the air praise you.
Let earth's wild beasts and the cattle of every field praise you.
For you are the God of all creation.

(from Prayer of Azariah)

(A time for reflection on the reading – silent or spoken)

Prayer

In the silence of our hearts or in spoken words
let us give thanks for the gift of this day
and pray for the life of the world . . .

(Here brief prayers may be offered)

In making the creatures, O God,
you called the senses into being
and named them as good.
In our tasting and touching,
in our smelling, hearing and seeing
may we be alive to the mystery of life
and alert to finding you in all things.

Closing Words
(after which candle is extinguished)

The blessings of heaven,
the blessings of earth,
the blessings of sea and of sky.
On those we love this day
and on every human family
the gifts of heaven,
the gifts of earth,
the gifts of sea and of sky.

DAY SIX
Opening Words
(as candle is lit)

We light a light
in the name of the God who creates life,
in the name of the Saviour who loves life,
in the name of the Spirit who is the fire of life.

*(Be still and aware of God's presence within
and all around)*

Scripture

On the sixth day God said, 'Let us make humankind in our image.'
So the wind grew strong over the swelling sea
and from the moist earth humanity was born.
Spirit and flesh were formed in the likeness of God.
Male and female came forth together.
And the words of heaven were spoken on earth,
'Be fruitful and multiply.
The earth is yours and you are the earth's,
the seeds, the seas, the creatures,
everything that has breath and every plant that grows.
Be strong in my likeness and guard the unity of life.'
God saw all that had been created and it was very good.
The relationship of earth and woman and man had begun.
And there was evening and morning, creation's sixth day.

(from Genesis 1)

Blessed are you in the whole earth, O God.
Let all the peoples praise you.
Let every nation sing your praise.
For you are the God of all creation.

(from Prayer of Azariah)

(A time for reflection on the reading – silent or spoken)

Prayer

In the silence of our hearts or in spoken words
let us give thanks for the gift of this day
and pray for the life of the world . . .

(Here brief prayers may be offered)

Made in your image,
formed in your likeness,
we carry your life within us, O God.
In every person, in every race,
in every nation on earth, O God,
we look for your presence and long for your peace.

Closing Words
(after which candle is extinguished)

The blessings of heaven,
the blessings of earth,
the blessings of sea and of sky.
On those we love this day
and on every human family
the gifts of heaven,
the gifts of earth,
the gifts of sea and of sky.

DAY SEVEN
Opening Words
(as candle is lit)

We light a light
in the name of the God who creates life,
in the name of the Saviour who loves life,
in the name of the Spirit who is the fire of life.

*(Be still and aware of God's presence within
and all around)*

Scripture

On the seventh day there was silence in heaven.
The mighty wind of life was still.
The sea was calm.
The morning stars glistened.
And earth slept.
The work was finished.
Creation had been born.
And the Mother of all things rested.
It was a holy day.
The heavens and the earth were well.
God saw its fullness.
And there was evening and morning, creation's seventh day.

(from Genesis 2)

Blessed are you in the temple of creation, O God.
Blessed are you in the heights of heaven.
Let all your works praise you.
Let the angels of light and the messengers of life sing your praise.
For you are the God of all creation.

(from Prayer of Azariah)

(A time for reflection on the reading – silent or spoken)

Prayer

In the silence of our hearts or in spoken words
let us give thanks for the gift of this day
and pray for the life of the world . . .

(Here brief prayers may be offered)

For rest in the night and the day's busyness,
for the silence of the winter earth
followed by spring's energy and summer's fruiting,
thanks be to you, O God.
In the pattern of the seasons,
in the rhythm of our days,
show us the stillness that renews life,
the letting go that deepens our strength of soul.

Closing Words
(after which candle is extinguished)

The blessings of heaven,
the blessings of earth,
the blessings of sea and of sky.
On those we love this day
and on every human family
the gifts of heaven,
the gifts of earth,
the gifts of sea and of sky.

BOOK TWO

Journey and Promise

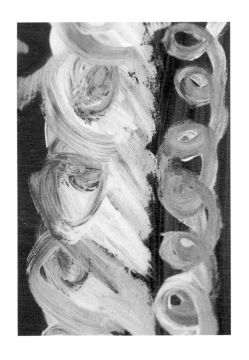

DAY ONE
Opening Words
(as candle is lit)

We light a light
in the name of the God who creates life,
in the name of the Saviour who loves life,
in the name of the Spirit who is the fire of life.

*(Be still and aware of God's presence within
and all around)*

Scripture

When the heavens and the earth were formed
God made a garden in the east called Eden.
In the garden there were trees of every kind
delightful to the senses and good for food.
And a river flowed out of Eden
branching to the north and south, the east and west.
Animals drank from its goodness, birds washed in its waters.
And on the banks of Eden's river God placed humankind.
The man was called Adam because he came from the ground.
And the woman was Eve for from her womb all human life would flow.
They lived and loved in the garden and were naked and not ashamed.
But also in Eden was the serpent.
He clothed himself with cunning and covered truth with lies.
'The tree that grows in the middle of the garden', he said,
'is forbidden but it is sweet to the taste. Eat of it. It is of God.
You will not die. It will make you wise, knowing good and evil.'
So the man and the woman were tricked by the twisting serpent.
They touched and tasted the forbidden fruit.
It did not kill them but their innocence in the garden had died.
Even what was good in them could now be twisted.
They saw their nakedness and were ashamed and covered themselves.
They hid from God and fled from the garden.
They remembered its goodness but lived in exile.

(from Genesis 2–3)

(A time for reflection on the reading – silent or spoken)

Prayer

In the silence of our hearts or in spoken words
let us give thanks for the gift of this day
and pray for the life of the world . . .

(Here brief prayers may be offered)

Our beginnings are in Eden, O God;
our genesis is in you.
Open to us the gateways of your presence in life
and the doors that lead us further into your mystery.
Awaken our memory of the garden of our beginnings
that we may find ourselves again in you.

Closing Words
(after which candle is extinguished)

The blessings of heaven,
the blessings of earth,
the blessings of sea and of sky.
On those we love this day
and on every human family
the gifts of heaven,
the gifts of earth,
the gifts of sea and of sky.

DAY TWO
Opening Words
(as candle is lit)

We light a light
in the name of the God who creates life,
in the name of the Saviour who loves life,
in the name of the Spirit who is the fire of life.

*(Be still and aware of God's presence within
and all around)*

Scripture

Eve, the mother of all the living, gave birth to a child.
There were tears of joy and pain at the birth.
And her children also had children and they too knew sorrow and delight.
After many generations there was Abraham and Sarah who were childless.
But in a dream God came to Abraham and said, 'Do not be afraid.
Look to heaven and count the stars. So shall your family be.
And in you all the people of the earth shall be blessed.'
Abraham believed God and yet for many years nothing happened.
Finally, when he was an old man sitting alone by his tent
three messengers of God appeared to him.
Abraham invited them to rest under the shade of his tree.
He washed their feet and gave them bread to eat and milk to drink.
'Where is Sarah your wife?' asked one of the visitors.
'She is in the tent,' replied Abraham. 'Why do you ask?'
'Because when I return to you next season,' said the messenger,
'Sarah shall have a son.'
Now Sarah had been listening at the entrance to the tent.
So she laughed to herself, 'At such an age shall I bear a child?'
And the messenger said, 'Why does Sarah laugh?
Is anything too wonderful for God?'
Sarah did conceive and the next season she gave birth to a son.
They called him Isaac which means laughter.
'God has brought laughter for me,' said Sarah.
'Everyone who hears will laugh with me.'
The child grew and became strong and through him a nation was born.

(from Genesis 15–21)

(A time for reflection on the reading – silent or spoken)

Prayer

In the silence of our hearts or in spoken words
let us give thanks for the gift of this day
and pray for the life of the world . . .

(Here brief prayers may be offered)

Hope and fear, laughter and tears have been part of our journey.
Joy and pain, longing and doubt meet on the pathway.
Often we do not believe, O God,
and sometimes we doubt that your promises can be true.
Grant us and our world the freedom to laugh, the courage to cry,
the heart to be open and the faith to believe.

Closing Words
(after which candle is extinguished)

The blessings of heaven,
the blessings of earth,
the blessings of sea and of sky.
On those we love this day
and on every human family
the gifts of heaven,
the gifts of earth,
the gifts of sea and of sky.

DAY THREE

Opening Words
(as candle is lit)

We light a light
in the name of the God who creates life,
in the name of the Saviour who loves life,
in the name of the Spirit who is the fire of life.

*(Be still and aware of God's presence within
and all around)*

Scripture

Isaac, the promised son of Abraham and Sarah, married Rebekah.
She was a beautiful woman who as a girl had lived by a fresh spring
  of water.
Isaac loved her and she gave birth to twin boys, Esau and Jacob.
But when they grew up Esau began to hate Jacob.
And Rebekah, afraid that she would lose both her sons if they fought,
sent Jacob away to a distant land until Esau could forget his anger.
As Jacob journeyed he came one night to an open place under
  the stars.
He lay down to sleep and as he slept he dreamt of a ladder.
Its top touched the heavens and its base rested on the earth.
Angels of God travelled up and down the ladder.
And one of the angels stood beside him and said,
'Know that I am with you and will keep you wherever you go.
I will never leave you and will bring you back to this land.'
Then Jacob woke from his sleep and said,
'God is in this place and I did not know it.
This is the gate of heaven and I am in the presence of God.'
So he called the place Bethel, which means House of God.
Many years later God did bring Jacob back.
He returned with family and treasure, with camels and cattle.
But in the night Jacob worried about meeting his brother
  the next day.
He wrestled with his fears and with the angel of God who
  was leading him.
They struggled through the night until the break of day.
And Jacob said to the angel, 'I will not let you go unless you bless me.'

So the angel replied, 'You will no longer be called Jacob but Israel,
for you have wrestled with God and survived.'
And the angel blessed him but from that day Jacob walked with
a limp for he had been wounded in his struggle with the angel.
When the day's light had fully broken Jacob looked and saw his
brother coming.
Esau ran to him and kissed him and together they wept.
And Jacob said to his brother, 'Seeing your face is like seeing
the face of God,
for you have welcomed me back with love.'

(*from Genesis 28–33*)

(*A time for reflection on the reading – silent or spoken*)

Prayer

In the silence of our hearts or in spoken words
let us give thanks for the gift of this day
and pray for the life of the world . . .

(Here brief prayers may be offered)

Let us dream of the angels that connect heaven and earth.
Let us imagine the threads of the eternal woven into time.
And let us know you among us now, O God.
In this time and every time may we know your blessings among us.

Closing Words

(after which candle is extinguished)

The blessings of heaven,
the blessings of earth,
the blessings of sea and of sky.
On those we love this day
and on every human family
the gifts of heaven,
the gifts of earth,
the gifts of sea and of sky.

DAY FOUR
Opening Words
(as candle is lit)

We light a light
in the name of the God who creates life,
in the name of the Saviour who loves life,
in the name of the Spirit who is the fire of life.

*(Be still and aware of God's presence within
and all around)*

Scripture

Jacob remained in the land along with Rachel whom he loved.
They prospered and grew as a family but still there were times of struggle.
Among their children was Joseph whom they especially loved.
He was the unexpected child of their older years.
Yet Joseph's brothers were jealous and secretly sold him into slavery.
Many years passed and Joseph remained a servant in Egypt.
But Pharaoh, the king of the land, had a dream that troubled him.
He saw seven fat cows eating happily in a field by the river.
And out of the water came seven thin cows who ate up the fat cows.
But no one in his court could help him with the dream.
So Joseph the son of Israel was sent for.
He was young but he was wise and said to the king,
'The seven fat cows are seven years of plenty.
And the seven thin cows are seven years of hunger.
The years of hunger will eat up the land.'
And so the king was taught by a slave.
Egypt prepared for the famine and its people were fed.
A golden chain was hung around Joseph's neck,
and the king placed power in the young man's hands.
Egypt survived the hungry years but other nations suffered.
They flocked to Pharaoh's court for help.
Among the hungry were the brothers of Joseph who had betrayed him.
When he saw them he wept over them
and they were frightened but he forgave them.
'Do not be afraid,' he said. 'God sent me ahead of you to save life.'
Joseph's family joined him in Egypt and they survived the years of famine.

(from Genesis 37–50)

(A time for reflection on the reading – silent or spoken)

Prayer

In the silence of our hearts or in spoken words
let us give thanks for the gift of this day
and pray for the life of the world . . .

(Here brief prayers may be offered)

You speak to us in all things, O God,
in the rising of the sun and its setting,
in dreams of the night and the encounters of day.
Let us know you in the whole of life,
in both the blessings and the betrayals of our lives.
Heal our hurts and open our hearts
that as families and nations we may be faithful to one another.

Closing Words
(after which candle is extinguished)

The blessings of heaven,
the blessings of earth,
the blessings of sea and of sky.
On those we love this day
and on every human family
the gifts of heaven,
the gifts of earth,
the gifts of sea and of sky.

DAY FIVE
Opening Words
(as candle is lit)

We light a light
in the name of the God who creates life,
in the name of the Saviour who loves life,
in the name of the Spirit who is the fire of life.

*(Be still and aware of God's presence within
and all around)*

Scripture

Joseph, the son of Israel and Rachel, lived in Egypt until he died.
His people, called the Hebrews, grew in number and in strength.
But a new Pharaoh became king in the land.
He did not remember the good that Joseph had done for Egypt
and he was frightened by how strong the Hebrew people
had become.
So he treated them like slaves and made their lives hard with
heavy work.
He ordered his soldiers to drown the newborn sons of Israel
in the river.
Hebrew mothers would hide their babies and the king's men
would find them.
Egypt became a land of deep wrong and sorrow.
But there was one woman who hid her boy in a basket by
the riverside.
It was a place where the king's daughter often bathed.
She was a brave princess and when she found the boy she took him
as her own.
She called him Moses, which means 'taken out of the water'.
So Moses grew up as a son of the royal palace.
And like the princess before him he was brave but he was rash.
In anger at the wrongs done to his people he killed one of the
king's men.
Then in fear for his life he fled from Pharaoh's court into the
wilderness.
There he lived in exile as a shepherd.
But beyond the wilderness there was a mountain called Horeb.

It was the mountain of God.
As Moses led his flock up Horeb an angel of fire appeared to him
    in a bush and a voice spoke to him from the heart of the flame,
'I am the God of Abraham and Sarah, of Isaac and Rebekah, Jacob
    and Rachel. Take off your shoes, for the place in which you are
    standing is holy ground.'
And Moses turned away his face, for he was afraid to look into
    God's presence.
'What is your name?', asked Moses.
And God answered him, 'I am beyond every name. I am what I am.
I have seen your people's suffering and I have heard your
    people's cry.
I am your freedom and your deliverance.
Go and tell Pharaoh to let the people go.'

(from Exodus 1–3)

(A time for reflection on the reading – silent or spoken)

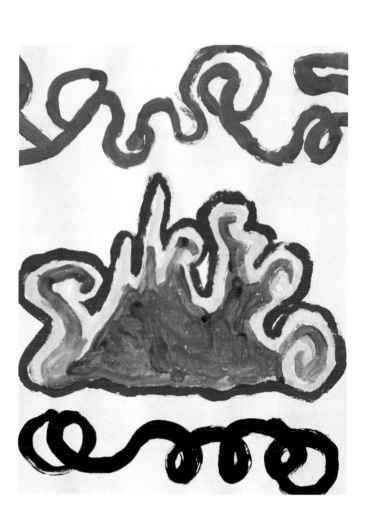

Prayer

In the silence of our hearts or in spoken words
let us give thanks for the gift of this day
and pray for the life of the world . . .

(Here brief prayers may be offered)

O God of our mothers and fathers
and of all who have gone before us
from every race and from every nation,
you are forever among us
as the One who makes this place and every place holy.
Let us know you here that we may look for your presence
  everywhere.
Let us know you now that we may be seekers of your freedom
  in the world.

Closing Words

(after which candle is extinguished)

The blessings of heaven,
the blessings of earth,
the blessings of sea and of sky.
On those we love this day
and on every human family
the gifts of heaven,
the gifts of earth,
the gifts of sea and of sky.

DAY SIX
Opening Words
(as candle is lit)

We light a light
in the name of the God who creates life,
in the name of the Saviour who loves life,
in the name of the Spirit who is the fire of life.

*(Be still and aware of God's presence within
and all around)*

Scripture

Moses returned to Egypt to lead his people from slavery into
    freedom.
He told Pharaoh, the king of the land, to let the Hebrew people go.
But the king's heart was hard and he became even more cruel.
He called the slaves lazy and had them beaten as they worked.
So Moses warned the king that his country would suffer if he did
    not change.
Darkness settled over the land.
The east wind brought clouds of grasshoppers that ate everything
    before them.
Nothing green was left growing in the fields but still the king's heart
    was closed.
Thunder, lightning and hailstones crashed down from the skies.
Tens of thousands of water creatures emerged from the flooding
    rivers.
Frogs swarmed the royal palace, toads slept in the king's bed,
tadpoles lined the kitchen cupboards and slime covered the castle
    floors.
And the magicians of the court could do nothing.
Finally, after even more disasters, the king relented, saying,
    'Let the slaves go.'
So Moses and the Hebrew people began their march to freedom.
Men and women, young and old, cattle and sheep journeyed
    together.
An angel of light travelled before them in a cloud by day and a
    flame by night.
It led them to the Sea of Reeds, where they paused to rest.

But Pharaoh's heart again was hardened and he came out to
capture them.
Horses and chariots, riders and foot-soldiers raced after the
Hebrew slaves.
But the cloud of God moved between them
and a mist separated Pharaoh's army from the fleeing slaves.
Moses stretched out his hand over the sea
and an angel of the east drove the waters back with a mighty
wind.
By early morning the sea had become dry land and the slaves
crossed in safety.
Pharaoh's army followed but the angel of God confused them.
Chariot wheels became clogged with mud and horses began to
panic.
Moses again stretched out his hand over the sea.
And from the west the dark waters returned.
Waves washed away Pharaoh's chariots and his soldiers sank
in the sea.
On the far shore of the waters Moses and the people stood free.
And Miriam, Moses' sister, led the women in a dance.

(from Exodus 5–15)

(A time for reflection on the reading – silent or spoken)

Prayer

In the silence of our hearts or in spoken words
let us give thanks for the gift of this day
and pray for the life of the world . . .

(Here brief prayers may be offered)

For mighty winds that sweep across the seas
and your mighty Spirit that disturbs the waters of life,
   thanks be to you, O God.
For the spirit of freedom that stirs our passions
and the longings for liberty that surge from human depths,
   thanks be to you.
Within us, between us and among us in our world
   hear the cry of earth's bound people.
Within us, between us and among us, O God,
   hear earth's cry for liberty.

Closing Words

(after which candle is extinguished)

The blessings of heaven,
the blessings of earth,
the blessings of sea and of sky.
On those we love this day
and on every human family
the gifts of heaven,
the gifts of earth,
the gifts of sea and of sky.

DAY SEVEN
Opening Words
(as candle is lit)

We light a light
in the name of the God who creates life,
in the name of the Saviour who loves life,
in the name of the Spirit who is the fire of life.

*(Be still and aware of God's presence within
and all around)*

Scripture

Freed from slavery Moses and his people began a long journey.
Ahead of them were deserts and mountains
and within them were doubts and fears.
For the first three days they found no water
until they came to a desert garden of twelve springs and seventy
  palm trees.
And there they were refreshed.
God still led them in a cloud of brightness
but soon they were without food and complained to Moses,
'Why did you not leave us in Egypt where we had our fill of bread
  and drink?
Instead you have led us into this wilderness to die.'
But God assured Moses in a vision saying,
'I will rain down bread from heaven and food from the skies.
And the people will have what they need'.
So a wind from God blew birds from afar and dropped them in
  the desert.
In the evenings there was meat enough for all.
And as the morning dews lifted there was grain on the ground like
  fine frost.
The people called it manna and its taste was like wafers with honey.
But the wilderness brought many trials for the people.
They lost their way and were confused. They quarrelled and became
  unsure.
So Moses climbed the cliffs of Sinai to seek the strength of God.
The holy mountain was covered with mist but Moses entered its
  darkness.

And there he cried, 'Be with me, O God, and show me your
    presence.'
From the heart of the cloud God answered Moses,
'My presence will always be with you but you cannot see my face.
For no one sees my face and lives.'
Moses remained on the mountain for forty days and forty nights.
When he came down the skin of his face shone, for he had been
    with God.
And he shared with his people words from Sinai to guide them on
    their journey.
They were words of life and death, of blessings and of warnings.
'Choose life,' he said, 'that you and your children may live'.
Moses did not enter the land of promise with his people
but he saw it from afar as an old man from the top of a mountain.
And he saw that it was a land of abundance, full of grain
    and wine.

(from Exodus 15–16, 33–34 and Deuteronomy 30–34)

(A time for reflection on the reading – silent or spoken)

Prayer

In the silence of our hearts or in spoken words
let us give thanks for the gift of this day
and pray for the life of the world . . .

(Here brief prayers may be offered)

We stumble on the journey, O God.
We lose heart along the way.
We forget your promises and blame one another.
Refresh us with the springs of your spirit in our souls
and open our senses to your guiding presence
that we may be part of the world's healing this day,
that we may be part of the world's healing.

Closing Words
(after which candle is extinguished)

The blessings of heaven,
the blessings of earth,
the blessings of sea and of sky.
On those we love this day
and on every human family
the gifts of heaven,
the gifts of earth,
the gifts of sea and of sky.

BOOK THREE

Power and Justice

DAY ONE
Opening Words
(as candle is lit)

We light a light
in the name of the God who creates life,
in the name of the Saviour who loves life,
in the name of the Spirit who is the fire of life.

*(Be still and aware of God's presence within
and all around)*

Scripture

After many years in the land of promise
the Hebrew people chose to have kings and queens to rule over them.
One of the first kings was David the son of Jesse from Bethlehem.
He was handsome with beautiful eyes and ruddy cheeks.
As a young man he had fought against Goliath the giant.
Goliath's people had come to make war on David's people.
They met in a valley with a mountain on either side.
Goliath stepped forward wearing a coat of armour
and in his hand was a sword of iron.
He shouted across the valley to the Hebrew army,
'Choose a warrior from among yourselves who will come and fight me.
If he wins we will serve your people but if I win you will be our slaves.'
The Hebrew soldiers were terrified by the threats of the giant.
But young David went out to fight Goliath.
He carried nothing in his hands but a sling and five smooth stones.
When the giant saw such a youth coming out to meet him he laughed.
'I will cut up your flesh and throw it to the birds,' he said.
But David answered him, 'I am not afraid of you.
You have come out with a sword and heavy shield.
But this battle is God's and God does not fight with swords and shields.'
David then slung one of the stones and struck the giant in the forehead.
And Goliath fell face down on the ground.
David ran towards him and with Goliath's own sword cut off his head.
When the enemy soldiers saw this they fled in fear.
And young David became a hero in Israel.

(from 1 Samuel 17)

(A time for reflection on the reading – silent or spoken)

Prayer

In the silence of our hearts or in spoken words
let us give thanks for the gift of this day
and pray for the life of the world . . .

(Here brief prayers may be offered)

You are our strength and salvation, O God.
You are our hope and deliverer.
In the midst of fear and uncertainty in our lives
and when the powerless of the world are overwhelmed by
  mighty forces
recall us to our true source of help.
Awaken us again to your strong presence within us.
Awaken us again to hope.

Closing Words
(after which candle is extinguished)

The blessings of heaven,
the blessings of earth,
the blessings of sea and of sky.
On those we love this day
and on every human family
the gifts of heaven,
the gifts of earth,
the gifts of sea and of sky.

DAY TWO
Opening Words
(as candle is lit)

We light a light
in the name of the God who creates life,
in the name of the Saviour who loves life,
in the name of the Spirit who is the fire of life.

(Be still and aware of God's presence within
and all around)

Scripture

David became one of the greatest kings of Israel.
He was a brave soldier and was loved by the people.
He made Jerusalem his capital and the nation became strong.
He wrote songs of joy and sadness but he was not always wise.
In the spring one year when his army went out to battle David
  stayed at home.
In the afternoons he would walk in his palace gardens and look
  out over the city.
One day he saw from his rooftop a woman bathing.
She was very beautiful and her name was Bathsheba.
She was married to one of David's officers
but the king instructed his messengers to bring her to him.
When Bathsheba entered the palace David loved her and
  lay with her.
In the morning he sent a letter to the general who was leading his
  army in battle.
He told him to send Bathsheba's husband into the fiercest fighting
and then to draw back suddenly so that he would be surrounded
  and killed.
Thus King David betrayed one of his bravest officers
and took the widow Bathsheba as his wife.
But there was a prophet in the land named Nathan.
He learned of what the king had done
and went to the palace to tell the king a story.
'Once there were two men who lived in a certain city,' he said.
  'The one was rich and had many sheep.
The other was poor and had only a lamb.

But in his greed the rich man stole the poor man's lamb.'
When David heard the story he said,
'How terrible! The rich man surely deserves to die.'
And Nathan said to David, 'You are that man.
God made you king of Israel and has given you fame and fortune.
There is nothing you could not have had.
Instead you have stolen another man's wife and killed a loyal
    soldier.'
Nathan's words of truth struck David like an arrow
and he lay all night on the ground and prayed with sorrow.
In the morning the prophet said, 'God has put away your sin.
    You shall not die.'
And Bathsheba bore David a son and they called him Solomon.

(from 2 Samuel 11–12)

(A time for reflection on the reading – silent or spoken)

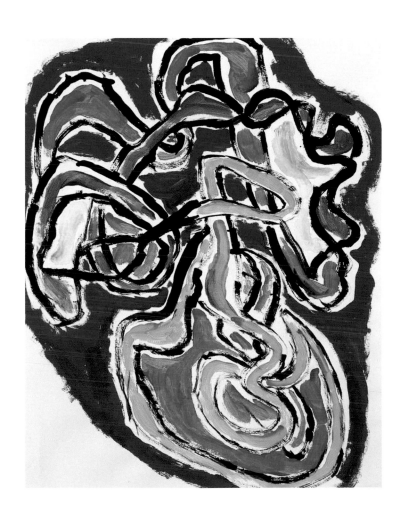

Prayer

In the silence of our hearts or in spoken words
let us give thanks for the gift of this day
and pray for the life of the world . . .

(Here brief prayers may be offered)

For the gift of life,
of our life and each life,
thanks be to you, O God.
Open our hearts to gratitude.
Free our minds from greed.
Heal our lives with grace.
And awaken our souls again to generosity.

Closing Words

(after which candle is extinguished)

The blessings of heaven,
the blessings of earth,
the blessings of sea and of sky.
On those we love this day
and on every human family
the gifts of heaven,
the gifts of earth,
the gifts of sea and of sky.

DAY THREE
Opening Words
(as candle is lit)

We light a light
in the name of the God who creates life,
in the name of the Saviour who loves life,
in the name of the Spirit who is the fire of life.

*(Be still and aware of God's presence within
and all around)*

Scripture

After David there were many kings and queens of Israel.
There were some who were strong and lived long.
And there were others who were false and deserted the people.
There was Uzziah who became king when he was sixteen.
Although he was young he learned to lead the nation
but in later years he became proud and neglected the needy.
So the prophet Amos, who was a shepherd, spoke against the king,
'The One who creates the stars and the planets
who turns the darkness of night into the light of day
and the light of day into the darkness of night
calls you to change.
Seek good and turn from evil that you may live.'
And Amos spoke out also against the friends and advisers of the king
who despised the poor and pushed them aside in the city streets,
'The One who creates the mountains and the earth
who turns the calm sea into storm and stormy seas into still waters
calls you to change.
Hate what is wrong and love what is good that you and the nation may live.'
And to the religious who practised prayer more than compassion
and loved festivities more than fairness, Amos said,
'I hate your festivals and despise your songs.
Instead let justice roll down like waters
and righteousness like an everflowing stream.'
But the nation did not change and its soul began to die.

(from Amos 5)

(A time for reflection on the reading – silent or spoken)

Prayer

In the silence of our hearts or in spoken words
let us give thanks for the gift of this day
and pray for the life of the world . . .

(Here brief prayers may be offered)

Lover of the poor,
defender of the needy,
sanctuary of the rejected:
for those who suffer injustice today,
for men and women who cannot provide food for their families,
and for whole communities who fear today and have no hope
   for tomorrow,
we offer the longings of our hearts in prayer.
We seek for them, O God, the gifts that are dear to us:
food for the table,
drink for the soul,
shelter in the night
and open arms to welcome us.

Closing Words
(after which candle is extinguished)

The blessings of heaven,
the blessings of earth,
the blessings of sea and of sky.
On those we love this day
and on every human family
the gifts of heaven,
the gifts of earth,
the gifts of sea and of sky.

DAY FOUR
Opening Words
(as candle is lit)

We light a light
in the name of the God who creates life,
in the name of the Saviour who loves life,
in the name of the Spirit who is the fire of life.

*(Be still and aware of God's presence within
and all around)*

Scripture

In the year that King Uzziah died another prophet began to speak.
His name was Isaiah and he spoke words of vision and comfort.
God will never forsake the heart of the people, he said.
'Thus says the One who created you
and formed you in your mother's womb.
Do not fear for I am your Strength.
I have called you by name and you are mine.
When you pass through deep waters I will be with you.
When you walk through fire I will guide you.
You are precious in my sight and I love you.
Do not be afraid for I am with you.
And do not dwell on what is past
for I am about to do a new thing.
It is coming now.
Do you not see it?
I will make your wilderness like Eden
and your desert like the garden of delight.
I will never forsake you or forget you.
And I will remember your sins no more.
Can a mother forget the babe at her breast
or hate the child of her own womb?
Even these may forget
but I will not forget you.'

(from Isaiah 43, 49)

(A time for reflection on the reading – silent or spoken)

Prayer

In the silence of our hearts or in spoken words
let us give thanks for the gift of this day
and pray for the life of the world . . .

(Here brief prayers may be offered)

All things come from you, O God:
the light of the rising sun and the enfolding darkness of night,
the lives of those who have gone before and the life of creatures
   still to be born.
As you blessed us at the beginning of time in the eternal womb of
   creation,
so bless us at the end of time when we journey into the unknown.
As you graced us with love at the dawn of this day,
so guide us and the world this night into the unfolding
   of tomorrow.

Closing Words
(after which candle is extinguished)

The blessings of heaven,
the blessings of earth,
the blessings of sea and of sky.
On those we love this day
and on every human family
the gifts of heaven,
the gifts of earth,
the gifts of sea and of sky.

DAY FIVE
Opening Words
(as candle is lit)

We light a light
in the name of the God who creates life,
in the name of the Saviour who loves life,
in the name of the Spirit who is the fire of life.

*(Be still and aware of God's presence within
and all around)*

Scripture

One of the most powerful enemies of Israel was the empire of
  the Assyrians.
Their greatest general led a mighty army to capture the Hebrew people.
There were hundreds of chariots and thousands of archers on
  horseback.
They surrounded the small army of Israel in a fortress town in the hills.
The springs that fed the fortress were seized and all the water supplies
  were cut off.
After thirty-four days every jar and flask of water in the town was
  empty.
Children and old people were collapsing in the streets.
And the Hebrew families feared that it would be better to surrender
than to see their little ones dying of thirst before them.
But also in the town was a woman of vision and of great courage.
She believed that God would free them from their enemy.
Her name was Judith.
She was a young widow known for a true heart and for her beauty
  of spirit.
During evening prayer when the incense was lit in the temple,
  she prayed,
'O God, your strength does not depend on numbers
nor does your might rely on the powerful.
You are the God of the weak and the oppressed.
You are the Saviour of those without hope.
O God of my mother and father,
Creator of heaven and earth,
hear the longings of my heart.'

Judith then removed her garments of mourning,
bathed herself in water,
anointed her body with scented oils,
placed a precious jewel around her neck
and clothed herself with festive colour.
Through the gates of the fortress she left the town
and crossed the valley to the enemy camp.
There she asked to speak with the Assyrian general.
When he saw her beauty and heard her speech
he desired her and sought to be alone with her.
Together they spoke and ate and as they ate the general drank more
  and more.
By the end of the evening he was drunk and fell into a deep sleep.
Judith took the sword that hung above his bed and cut off his head.
Under the cover of night she slipped out of the camp into the hills.
At dawn the Assyrians discovered the dead body of their general.
Fear seized them and they fled in panic.
So the Hebrew people were freed from their enemy by the hand of
  a woman.
They danced in the streets and the women were crowned with
  olive wreaths.

(from Judith 1–15)

(A time for reflection on the reading – silent or spoken)

Prayer

In the silence of our hearts or in spoken words
let us give thanks for the gift of this day
and pray for the life of the world . . .

(Here brief prayers may be offered)

That hope is deeper than despair
and that creativity surges from unknown depths within us,
thanks be to you, O God.
In the world this day
and in the relationships of men and women everywhere
let there be new stirrings of your liberating Spirit.
In the world this day and in the depths of our own souls
let there be new stirrings of your mighty liberating Spirit.

Closing Words
(after which candle is extinguished)

The blessings of heaven,
the blessings of earth,
the blessings of sea and of sky.
On those we love this day
and on every human family
the gifts of heaven,
the gifts of earth,
the gifts of sea and of sky.

DAY SIX
Opening Words
(as candle is lit)

We light a light
in the name of the God who creates life,
in the name of the Saviour who loves life,
in the name of the Spirit who is the fire of life.

*(Be still and aware of God's presence within
and all around)*

Scripture

For many years the Hebrew people lived in safety.
But the royal family and leaders of the nation again forgot the way
    of justice.
The poor were neglected, innocent blood was shed and the land
    became weak.
A powerful enemy, the empire of the Babylonians, rose up against
    Israel.
Jerusalem was captured, the king and queen were taken into exile,
generals and warriors, artists and musicians all were bound and led
    into captivity.
Only the poorest of the poor were left.
The temple, the palace and every great house in the city was burned
and its high walls were torn down.
And far from home, by the rivers of Babylon,
the captives sat down and wept when they remembered Jerusalem.
But again there was a prophet.
His name was Jeremiah.
He had warned the nation of Israel that it was collapsing
but the leaders were deaf to his words.
In exile he still loved his people and spoke to them words of comfort
    from God:
'Keep your voice from weeping and your eyes from tears.
You shall come back from the land of your enemy.
There is hope for the future.
There is promise for your children.
I have loved you with an everlasting love
and will continue my faithfulness to you.

The city shall be rebuilt.
Again you will make music and sing.
Again you will plant vineyards and enjoy the fruit.
Your life shall become like a watered garden,
like a deep spring whose waters never fail.
Then shall your young women sing and dance
and young men and old shall be merry.
For the One who makes the sun shine by day
and the moon and stars glisten by night
will turn your mourning into joy and give you gladness instead
   of sorrow.'

(from Jeremiah 31)

(A time for reflection on the reading – silent or spoken)

Prayer

In the silence of our hearts or in spoken words
let us give thanks for the gift of this day
and pray for the life of the world . . .

(Here brief prayers may be offered)

O God of new beginnings,
who brings light out of night's darkness
and fresh green out of the hard winter earth,
there is barren land between us as people and as nations
    this day,
there are empty stretches of soul within us.
Give us eyes to see new dawnings of promise.
Give us ears to hear fresh soundings of birth.

Closing Words
(after which candle is extinguished)

The blessings of heaven,
the blessings of earth,
the blessings of sea and of sky.
On those we love this day
and on every human family
the gifts of heaven,
the gifts of earth,
the gifts of sea and of sky.

DAY SEVEN
Opening Words
(as candle is lit)

We light a light
in the name of the God who creates life,
in the name of the Saviour who loves life,
in the name of the Spirit who is the fire of life.

*(Be still and aware of God's presence within
and all around)*

Scripture

The Babylonian captivity of the Hebrews lasted for more than forty
  years.
Many died without seeing their homeland again.
And others gave up hope that their sorrow would ever be turned
  into gladness.
But one man believed.
He was the prophet Ezekiel.
In a dream he was shown a valley full of bones.
There were very many and they were very dry.
And in the dream the Spirit of God asked him, 'Can these bones live?'
Ezekiel answered, 'Only you know, O God.'
Then the Spirit said to him, 'Prophesy to these bones and say to them,
"I will cause breath to enter you and you shall live.
I will cause flesh and skin to cover you and you shall come back to
  life again."'
So Ezekiel spoke from God and suddenly there was a noise, a rattling,
and the bones came together, bone attached to bone.
But still there was no breath in them.
So the Spirit said, 'Prophesy and say, "Thus says God,
Come from the four winds, O breath,
and breathe upon these bones that they may live."'
So Ezekiel spoke from God and the breath came into them
and they lived and stood on their feet, a great number.
Then the Spirit said to Ezekiel, 'These bones are the house of Israel.
They say that their bones are dried up and that their hope is lost.
Therefore prophesy and say to them, "I am going to open your graves.
I am going to raise you from the pit of hopelessness.

And I am going to bring you back to your land.
I will breathe my spirit within you and you shall live
and I will place you on your own soil again." '
And it happened as Ezekiel had seen in his dream.
The empire of the Babylonians was defeated by the Persians
and the King of Persia let the Hebrew people go.
They returned to Jerusalem singing and the walls of the city were
   built up again.

(from Ezekiel 37)

(A time for reflection on the reading – silent or spoken)

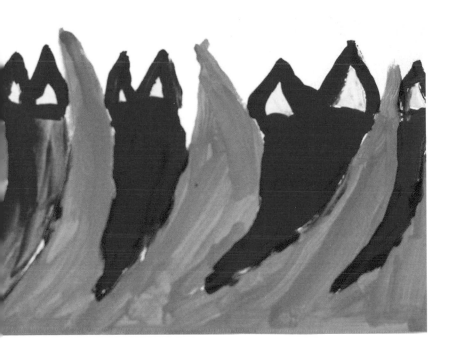

Prayer

In the silence of our hearts or in spoken words
let us give thanks for the gift of this day
and pray for the life of the world . . .

(Here brief prayers may be offered)

When it seemed there was no hope
you showed us new ways forward, O God.
When it seemed there were only endings
you showed us new beginnings.
Strengthen our belief in the power of life over death.
Strengthen our belief in the force of truth over falsehood
that we may be bearers of hope in the world,
that we may be bearers of hope.

Closing Words
(after which candle is extinguished)

The blessings of heaven,
the blessings of earth,
the blessings of sea and of sky.
On those we love this day
and on every human family
the gifts of heaven,
the gifts of earth,
the gifts of sea and of sky.

BOOK FOUR

Sayings of Wisdom

DAY ONE
Opening Words
(as candle is lit)

We light a light
in the name of the God who creates life,
in the name of the Saviour who loves life,
in the name of the Spirit who is the fire of life.

*(Be still and aware of God's presence within
and all around)*

Scripture

In every generation there are wise women and men.
They understand the human heart and speak words of truth.
They are remembered for their insights and cherished for their
  vision.
The Hebrew people especially remembered the wisdom of Solomon.
When he was a young king he had a dream that changed his life.
God came to him in the night and asked him what he most wanted.
'Give me understanding,' said Solomon, 'that I may be wise.
Allow me to know what is good and what is evil that I may care for
  the people.'
So God promised Solomon wisdom as well as wealth and a long life.
He became a man of great learning and knew what was in the
  human soul.
He studied art and music and designed a temple of wonder and
  beauty.
And though he built a holy place of prayer he knew that God was in
  every place.
'Even heaven and the highest heaven cannot contain you', he prayed,
'much less this temple that I have built.'
And so Solomon taught the people that God is greater than any place
and higher than any name or image that the human mind can create.
The nation grew under his wisdom and the people looked to him for
  justice.
On one occasion there were two women who came to Solomon with
  a quarrel.
The first woman said, 'We both live in the same house,
and we both had baby boys around the same time.

This woman's baby died last night while mine slept soundly at my
   breast.
But in the dark of the night she stole my son and placed hers at my
   side.
In the morning when I woke I thought my child was dead.
But when I looked more closely I saw that it was hers.'
The second woman responded, 'No, my lord, the living child is mine.'
The women argued and argued and no one in the court knew whom
   to believe.
So Solomon asked for a sword and ordered that the living boy be cut
   in two.
'Each woman can have half,' he said.
But the first woman cried out with tears, 'No, my lord, do not kill
   the child.
Give this woman my boy but please let him live.'
At this Solomon knew who the true mother was, for she loved
   her son.
So the king gave back the boy to the first woman
and the fame of Solomon's wisdom spread further through the land.
                        (*from 2 Chronicles 6 and 1 Kings 3*)

(A time for reflection on the reading – silent or spoken)

Prayer

In the silence of our hearts or in spoken words
let us give thanks for the gift of this day
and pray for the life of the world . . .

(Here brief prayers may be offered)

Heal our inner sight, O God,
that we may know the difference between good and evil.
Open our eyes
that we may see what is true and what is false.
Restore us to wisdom
that we may be well in our own souls.
Restore us to wisdom
that we and our world may be well.

Closing Words
(after which candle is extinguished)

The blessings of heaven,
the blessings of earth,
the blessings of sea and of sky.
On those we love this day
and on every human family
the gifts of heaven,
the gifts of earth,
the gifts of sea and of sky.

DAY TWO
Opening Words
(as candle is lit)

We light a light
in the name of the God who creates life,
in the name of the Saviour who loves life,
in the name of the Spirit who is the fire of life.

*(Be still and aware of God's presence within
and all around)*

Scripture

I will tell you what wisdom is and how she came to be
and will trace her path from the beginning of time.
I will make her teachings clear to you
and will not pass by the truth.
For the company of the wise is the salvation of the world
and those who love her receive great treasure.
Wisdom is radiant like the whiteness of the moon
and more beautiful than the glistening stars.
She is found by those who seek her
and makes herself known to those who long for her.
She can be found sitting at the gateways of life
in every moment and on every path.
She is a breath of the power of God and a pure flow of heaven's glory.
She is a reflection of eternal light and an image of God's goodness.
Wisdom was in the beginning with God.
She is creation's artist and the fashioner of everything that exists.
She loves right relationship and teaches justice and courage.
She knows the things of old and senses the things to come.
She understands all speech and can interpret every sign and wonder.
And so I loved her and sought her from my youth.
I chose her as my bride and have delighted in her presence.
For she is the everlasting gift of God.

(from Wisdom of Solomon 6–8)

(A time for reflection on the reading – silent or spoken)

Prayer

In the silence of our hearts or in spoken words
let us give thanks for the gift of this day
and pray for the life of the world . . .

(Here brief prayers may be offered)

The lights of the heavens were imagined by her.
The textures of earth were thought by her.
The power of the wind was her delight.
The creatures of earth, sea and sky were painted by her.
The senses of the body and appetites of the soul were named
   by her.
She was present at the birth of all things.
Renew us in your wisdom, O God,
for she is the midwife of our beginnings.

CELTIC TREASURE

118

Closing Words

(after which candle is extinguished)

The blessings of heaven,
the blessings of earth,
the blessings of sea and of sky.
On those we love this day
and on every human family
the gifts of heaven,
the gifts of earth,
the gifts of sea and of sky.

DAY THREE
Opening Words
(as candle is lit)

We light a light
in the name of the God who creates life,
in the name of the Saviour who loves life,
in the name of the Spirit who is the fire of life.

*(Be still and aware of God's presence within
and all around)*

Scripture

I prayed and understanding was given me.
I called on God and the spirit of wisdom came to me.
I preferred her to chariots and thrones
and knew that riches and wealth did not compare with wisdom.
All gold is but a little sand in her sight and silver is like clay beside her.
But wisdom is not ours unless God gives her to us.
It is a mark of understanding to know whose gift she is.
So I prayed with my whole heart and pleaded with all my soul:
'O God of our mothers and fathers,
O Giver of every good gift and fountain of mercy,
you formed humanity in your likeness,
you spoke all things into being,
send forth wisdom from the highest heaven
that she may labour at my side and I may learn what is pleasing to you.
For she knows and understands all things
and will guide me wisely in my actions.
You are merciful to all, O God.
You renew all things.
You forgive our sins that we may grow in truth.
You hate nothing that lives.
Creation would not have been born if you had not blessed it.
Your ever-living spirit is in all things for they are yours.
O You who love the living,
grant me wisdom that I may find friendship with you.'

(from Wisdom of Solomon 9–11)

(A time for reflection on the reading – silent or spoken)

Prayer

In the silence of our hearts or in spoken words
let us give thanks for the gift of this day
and pray for the life of the world . . .

(Here brief prayers may be offered)

Open our eyes to see your Spirit in all life.
Open our hearts to receive the blessing that is in
    all created things.
Guide us with your wisdom, O God,
in the handling of matter,
in the sharing of earth's resources
and in the knowing of one another,
your Spirit within every living spirit.

Closing Words

(after which candle is extinguished)

The blessings of heaven,
the blessings of earth,
the blessings of sea and of sky.
On those we love this day
and on every human family
the gifts of heaven,
the gifts of earth,
the gifts of sea and of sky.

DAY FOUR
Opening Words
(as candle is lit)

We light a light
in the name of the God who creates life,
in the name of the Saviour who loves life,
in the name of the Spirit who is the fire of life.

*(Be still and aware of God's presence within
and all around)*

Scripture

Wisdom calls to us from the crossroads of life.
She raises her voice and says:
'To you, O people, I call. My words are to all who live.
Come to me, you who lack understanding.
Hear, for I will speak gracious things
and from my lips will come what is true and right.
Seek my teachings instead of silver and my knowledge rather than gold
for wisdom is better than jewels
and everything else you desire does not compare with her.
I, wisdom, will offer you awareness and strength of soul.
I walk in the way of right relationships and along the paths of peace.
I give knowledge and understanding to those who love me.
God created me at the beginning of time
long before the creation of heaven and earth.
When there were neither heights nor depths I was brought forth.
Before the mountains and hills were formed I was there.
When the moon and the sun were established,
when the sea and earth were filled with creatures,
I was beside God like a playful artist and daily God delighted in me.
I rejoice in the inhabited world. I love the human race.
So now, my children, listen to me.
Watch for me in the morning and wait for me at night.
Hear my guidance and be wise.
For those who find me find life but those who lose me will lose their way.'

(from Proverbs 8)

(A time for reflection on the reading – silent or spoken)

Prayer

In the silence of our hearts or in spoken words
let us give thanks for the gift of this day
and pray for the life of the world . . .

(Here brief prayers may be offered)

In the silence of our hearts we listen for wisdom, O God,
that we may learn again that we are born of you
and that all people are bearers of your everlasting image.
In the silence of our hearts we listen
that we may know once more that the earth and all its creatures
  are sacred
and that within us and among us is your wisdom and your
  delight.

Closing Words
(after which candle is extinguished)

The blessings of heaven,
the blessings of earth,
the blessings of sea and of sky.
On those we love this day
and on every human family
the gifts of heaven,
the gifts of earth,
the gifts of sea and of sky.

DAY FIVE
Opening Words
(as candle is lit)

We light a light
in the name of the God who creates life,
in the name of the Saviour who loves life,
in the name of the Spirit who is the fire of life.

*(Be still and aware of God's presence within
and all around)*

Scripture

Happy are you who meditate on wisdom,
who reflect in your heart on her ways
and ponder her secrets,
who listen for her on life's pathways
and look for her at every turn.
She will come to meet you like a mother
and like a young lover she will welcome you.
So listen to the counsel of your own heart
and above all pray to the Most High
that you may be guided in the way of truth.
For it is God who created humankind in the beginning
and gave us the power to choose freely.
It is God who wove into our hearts the voice of truth
and invites us to act faithfully.
Life and death stand before us at each moment
and whichever one we choose will be given.
Happy are those whose hearts do not condemn them
and who have not given up hope.
God searches the depths of the human spirit
and understands our innermost secrets.
Those who love wisdom love life
and whoever seeks her from early morning will be blessed.

(from Ecclesiasticus 14 -15)

(A time for reflection on the reading – silent or spoken)

Prayer

In the silence of our hearts or in spoken words
let us give thanks for the gift of this day
and pray for the life of the world . . .

(Here brief prayers may be offered)

For ourselves and for the world
we seek wisdom.
For ourselves and all people
we seek understanding.
For ourselves and the whole of creation
we seek your blessings, O God.

Closing Words

(after which candle is extinguished)

The blessings of heaven,
the blessings of earth,
the blessings of sea and of sky.
On those we love this day
and on every human family
the gifts of heaven,
the gifts of earth,
the gifts of sea and of sky.

DAY SIX
Opening Words
(as candle is lit)

We light a light
in the name of the God who creates life,
in the name of the Saviour who loves life,
in the name of the Spirit who is the fire of life.

*(Be still and aware of God's presence within
and all around)*

Scripture

God created human beings out of the earth
and makes us return to it again.
God gave us a fixed number of days
and invites us into relationship with everything that lives.
God blessed us with strength and beauty
and inspires us with everlasting hope.
God placed wisdom within us in our mother's womb
and shows us what is good and what is evil.
God commanded us to love our neighbour
and warns us to follow the law of unity.
Remember that it was of your parents that you were born.
How can you ever repay them?
With all your heart honour your father
and do not forget the birth pangs of your mother.
Stretch out your hand to the poor
so that you may grow in goodness and generosity.
Give graciously to all the living
and be merciful in how you speak even of the dead.
Do not avoid those who weep but mourn with those who mourn.
Do not hesitate to visit the sick because for such deeds you will be loved.
In all you do, look to the heart of life and you will be free from great sin.
And when you do fail, remember that God encourages all who
are losing hope.
There are new beginnings for those who seek forgiveness.

(from Ecclesiasticus 7 and 17)

(A time for reflection on the reading – silent or spoken)

Prayer

In the silence of our hearts or in spoken words
let us give thanks for the gift of this day
and pray for the life of the world . . .

(Here brief prayers may be offered)

In your forgiveness we seek new beginnings, O God.
In your generosity we seek what is best for one another.
In your grace we seek freedom from bitterness.
In your mercy we seek healing for the nations.

Closing Words
(after which candle is extinguished)

The blessings of heaven,
the blessings of earth,
the blessings of sea and of sky.
On those we love this day
and on every human family
the gifts of heaven,
the gifts of earth,
the gifts of sea and of sky.

DAY SEVEN
Opening Words
(as candle is lit)

We light a light
in the name of the God who creates life,
in the name of the Saviour who loves life,
in the name of the Spirit who is the fire of life.

*(Be still and aware of God's presence within
and all around)*

Scripture

Bless the God of all
who everywhere works great wonders
and by whose will all things are made.
The shining stars are the beauty of the universe,
a glittering array in the heights of God.
Look at the rainbow and praise the One who made it.
It stretches across the sky with its glorious arc.
By God's command lightning flashes from heaven
and thunder shakes the earth.
Cold snow blows from the north
and the south wind brings summer breezes.
The sun's heat scorches the wilderness
and withers the grass like fire.
Wet mist hovers between the mountains
and falling dews refresh the land.
The swelling sea is full of danger
and strange creatures crawl forth from its depths.
By heaven's word all things are created.
We could say more but could never say enough.
Let the final word be, 'God is in all things.'
So bless the God of all who everywhere works great wonders,
who watches over our life from birth to death
and deals with us mercifully.
May there be peace in our days
and may there be gladness in our hearts.
            (*from Ecclesiasticus 43, 50*)

(A time for reflection on the reading – silent or spoken)

Prayer

In the silence of our hearts or in spoken words
let us give thanks for the gift of this day
and pray for the life of the world . . .

(Here brief prayers may be offered)

O God of those who have gone before us,
O God of our children and those still to be born,
O God of creatures and all growing things,
O God of the heavens and the seasons,
of winter's barrenness and spring's energy,
of summer's fruiting and autumn's ripeness,
you are the God of all life.
May we know you and reverence you in all that lives.

Closing Words
(after which candle is extinguished)

The blessings of heaven,
the blessings of earth,
the blessings of sea and of sky.
On those we love this day
and on every human family
the gifts of heaven,
the gifts of earth,
the gifts of sea and of sky.

BOOK FIVE

Songs of the Soul

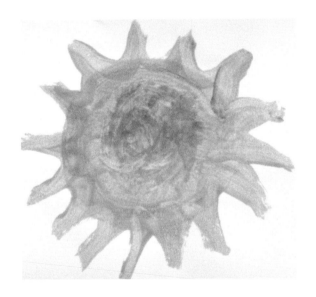

DAY ONE
Opening Words
(as candle is lit)

We light a light
in the name of the God who creates life,
in the name of the Saviour who loves life,
in the name of the Spirit who is the fire of life.

*(Be still and aware of God's presence within
and all around)*

Scripture

As a deer longs for flowing streams
so my soul longs for you, O God.
My soul thirsts for God,
for the living God.
When shall I glimpse your presence again?
My tears have become my food day and night
as people say to me, 'Where is your God?'
I remember how I sang and danced with others in the great temple,
how I led the festive crowds.
I remember the joy and the shouts of gladness.
These things I remember now as I pour out my soul.
Why are you cast down, O my soul,
and why are you troubled within me?
Hope in God, for I shall again find strength.
At the rising of the sun God's love streams forth.
In the darkness of the night a song still stirs within me.
It is a prayer to the God of my life.
I say to God, my rock, 'Why have you forgotten me?
Why is my heart so heavy?'
Hope in God, O my soul, for I shall again find strength,
my help and my God.

(from Psalm 42)

(A time for reflection on the reading – silent or spoken)

Prayer

In the silence of our hearts or in spoken words
let us give thanks for the gift of this day
and pray for the life of the world . . .

(Here brief prayers may be offered)

You have been our strength, O God.
At the beginning of the day you brought us from darkness
   into light.
At the ending of the day you lead us from busyness into stillness.
In earth's cycles and seasons you offer us new life and fresh
   beginnings.
Be our strength this day and the strength of new beginnings
   in our world.
Be our help, O God, and the help of those who cry out in need.

Closing Words

(after which candle is extinguished)

The blessings of heaven,
the blessings of earth,
the blessings of sea and of sky.
On those we love this day
and on every human family
the gifts of heaven,
the gifts of earth,
the gifts of sea and of sky.

DAY TWO
Opening Words
(as candle is lit)

We light a light
in the name of the God who creates life,
in the name of the Saviour who loves life,
in the name of the Spirit who is the fire of life.

*(Be still and aware of God's presence within
and all around)*

Scripture

God is our shelter and strength,
a very present help in trouble.
Therefore we will not be afraid
though the earth should change
though the mountains shake in the heart of the sea
though its waters roar and foam
though the mountains tremble with the shaking.
There is a river whose streams make glad the city of God,
the dwelling place of the Eternal.
God is in the midst of the city. It shall not be forsaken.
God will help it when the morning dawns.
The nations are in an uproar. The kingdoms totter.
God speaks and earth's powers melt away.
The God of heaven is present on earth.
The One who was in the beginning is now.
Come and see the works of God.
Look at how the mighty are brought down.
God makes wars come to an end throughout the world.
The bow is broken and the spear is shattered.
The sword and shield are burned with fire.
'Be still and know that I am God.
I am loved among the nations. I am loved throughout the earth.'
The God of heaven is present on earth.
The One who was in the beginning is now.

(from Psalm 46)

(A time for reflection on the reading – silent or spoken)

Prayer

In the silence of our hearts or in spoken words
let us give thanks for the gift of this day
and pray for the life of the world . . .

(Here brief prayers may be offered)

O God of heaven, you are present on earth.
O God of the stars and planets, you are in the midst of the city.
O God above all things, you are in the depths of our being.
The river of your eternal life runs through all things.
Let us be glad to be bearers of your eternity.
Let us be glad to find you in one another.

Closing Words
(after which candle is extinguished)

The blessings of heaven,
the blessings of earth,
the blessings of sea and of sky.
On those we love this day
and on every human family
the gifts of heaven,
the gifts of earth,
the gifts of sea and of sky.

DAY THREE
Opening Words
(as candle is lit)

We light a light
in the name of the God who creates life,
in the name of the Saviour who loves life,
in the name of the Spirit who is the fire of life.

*(Be still and aware of God's presence within
and all around)*

Scripture

Have mercy on me, O God, because of your love.
Because of your love, blot out my sins.
Wash me from my wrongdoings and cleanse me from my faults.
For I know my wickedness and my sin is ever before me.
Against you I have sinned and done what is false in your sight.
You are true in your judgements.
You are right when you name my failures.
I was born into a world of wrongdoing.
Even in my mother's womb I was affected by the world's wrongs.
You desire truth in the inward being.
Therefore show me wisdom in my secret heart.
Bathe me with herbs and spices and I shall be clean.
Wash me and I shall be whiter than snow.
Let me hear joy and gladness again
and let the song that has died in me live.
Hide your face from my sins and blot out my wrongs.
Create in me a clean heart, O God,
and place a right spirit within me.
Do not cast me away from your presence
and do not take your holy spirit from me.
Restore me to the joy of your salvation
and strengthen in me a generous heart.
Open my lips, O God, and my mouth will speak your praise.
For you delight in a true spirit and an open heart you will not despise.

(from Psalm 51)

(A time for reflection on the reading – silent or spoken)

Prayer

In the silence of our hearts or in spoken words
let us give thanks for the gift of this day
and pray for the life of the world . . .

(Here brief prayers may be offered)

Grant us open hearts, O God,
open to you
and open to one another,
open to the splendour of the earth
and open to its pain and the pain of its people.
Grant us open hearts, O God.

Closing Words

(after which candle is extinguished)

The blessings of heaven,
the blessings of earth,
the blessings of sea and of sky.
On those we love this day
and on every human family
the gifts of heaven,
the gifts of earth,
the gifts of sea and of sky.

DAY FOUR
Opening Words
(as candle is lit)

We light a light
in the name of the God who creates life,
in the name of the Saviour who loves life,
in the name of the Spirit who is the fire of life.

*(Be still and aware of God's presence within
and all around)*

Scripture

Give the leaders of the nations your justice, O God.
May they lead the people with truth and the poor with compassion.
May they defend the needy and stop the oppressor.
May they be wise as long as the sun and the moon shine.
May they be like rain that falls on dry ground,
like showers that water the earth.
In their days may right relationships thrive and peace prosper.
May they have power from sea to sea
and from the river to the ends of the earth.
May they pity the weak and save the sick,
for precious is the blood of the poor.
May prayers be said for them continually
and blessings offered all day long.
May there be plenty of grain in the land.
May it wave on the tops of the mountains
and bring health to every family.
May people blossom in the cities
and children grow like flowers of the field.
May their name and their fame last for ever.
May every nation of the world be blessed in them
and may they know happiness in their own lives.
Blessed be you, O God of all creation.
May your glory fill the earth.

(from Psalm 72)

(A time for reflection on the reading – silent or spoken)

Prayer

In the silence of our hearts or in spoken words
let us give thanks for the gift of this day
and pray for the life of the world . . .

(Here brief prayers may be offered)

Give us peace in our days, O God.
Let us live in harmony with one another.
Let us care for the earth and its creatures.
Let us be true as nations.
Let us guard one another's dignity.
And let us protect the peace that belongs to the whole
   of creation.

Closing Words
(after which candle is extinguished)

The blessings of heaven,
the blessings of earth,
the blessings of sea and of sky.
On those we love this day
and on every human family
the gifts of heaven,
the gifts of earth,
the gifts of sea and of sky.

DAY FIVE
Opening Words
(as candle is lit)

We light a light
in the name of the God who creates life,
in the name of the Saviour who loves life,
in the name of the Spirit who is the fire of life.

*(Be still and aware of God's presence within
and all around)*

Scripture

Blessed be God, O my soul and all that is within me,
blessed be God's holy name,
who forgives all our sins,
who heals all our diseases,
who saves our life from the pit,
who satisfies us with good as long as we live
so that our youth is renewed like the eagle's.
God liberates those who are oppressed
and defends those who are wronged.
God is merciful and gracious, slow to anger and firm in love.
God does not look at us through our sins
nor repay our falseness.
For as the heavens are high above the earth
so great is God's infinite love.
As far as the east is from the west
so far does God remove our wrongs from us.
As a mother has compassion for her children
so God has compassion for the children of earth.
The love of God is from everlasting to everlasting.
Heaven's faithfulness is from eternity to eternity.
Blessed be God, O you angels and messengers of heaven.
Blessed be God, O you creatures and families of earth.
Blessed be God, O my soul and all that is within me,
blessed be God's holy name.

(from Psalm 103)

(A time for reflection on the reading – silent or spoken)

Prayer

In the silence of our hearts or in spoken words
let us give thanks for the gift of this day
and pray for the life of the world . . .

(Here brief prayers may be offered)

For your goodness, O God, boundless and everlasting,
    thanks be to you.
For your generosity, gracious and wise, thanks be to you.
For your mercy, strong and free, thanks be to you.
Let us share your goodness.
Let us practise your generosity.
Let us live your mercy that we and the world may be well.

Closing Words
(after which candle is extinguished)

The blessings of heaven,
the blessings of earth,
the blessings of sea and of sky.
On those we love this day
and on every human family
the gifts of heaven,
the gifts of earth,
the gifts of sea and of sky.

DAY SIX

Opening Words

(as candle is lit)

We light a light
in the name of the God who creates life,
in the name of the Saviour who loves life,
in the name of the Spirit who is the fire of life.

*(Be still and aware of God's presence within
and all around)*

Scripture

You have searched me and known me, O God.
You know when I sit down and when I rise up.
You see my path and my lying down and are familiar with all my ways.
You enfold me before and behind, above and beneath.
Even before a word is on my lips you know it completely.
Such knowledge is too wonderful for me.
It is so great that I cannot grasp it.
Where can I go from your spirit or where shall I flee from your presence?
If I ascend to heaven you are there.
If I make my bed in hell you are there.
If I take the wings of the morning to the farthest limits of the sea,
even there your hand shall guide me and your arm shall hold me close.
If I say, 'Let the daylight become night so that darkness may cover me',
even the veil of night will not hide me, for darkness is as light to you.
It was you who formed my inward parts.
You knit me together in my mother's womb.
I praise you for I am fearfully and wonderfully made.
In your book were written the days that were formed for me
even when none of them yet existed.
I sleep and I wake, I am born and I die, and always I am still with you.
Search me, O God, and know my heart.
Test me and know my thoughts.
See if there is any wickedness in me and lead me in the way everlasting.

(from Psalm 139)

(A time for reflection on the reading – silent or spoken)

Prayer

In the silence of our hearts or in spoken words
let us give thanks for the gift of this day
and pray for the life of the world . . .

(Here brief prayers may be offered)

You know what is within us, O God.
You know the beauty and the falseness of our hearts.
You know the heights and depths of the human spirit.
Lead us further into the universe of our souls
that we may know the wisdom and strength that you have
    placed within us.
Lead us further into the mystery of our souls
that we may be strong and wise for the well-being of the world.

Closing Words

(after which candle is extinguished)

The blessings of heaven,
the blessings of earth,
the blessings of sea and of sky.
On those we love this day
and on every human family
the gifts of heaven,
the gifts of earth,
the gifts of sea and of sky.

DAY SEVEN
Opening Words
(as candle is lit)

We light a light
in the name of the God who creates life,
in the name of the Saviour who loves life,
in the name of the Spirit who is the fire of life.

*(Be still and aware of God's presence within
and all around)*

Scripture

Happy are those whose help is the God of all creation,
who keeps faith for ever,
who demands justice for the oppressed,
who gives food to the hungry,
who sets the prisoners free
and opens the eyes of the blind,
who watches over the stranger
and upholds the widow and orphan,
who lifts up those who are broken
and brings down the proud and the wicked.
Praise God in the heavens.
Praise God in the heights.
Praise God, all you angels.
Praise God, sun and moon.
Praise God from the earth,
you sea-monsters and creatures of the deep,
fire and hail, snow and frost, stormy winds and scorching heat,
mountains and hills, fruit trees and towering pines,
wild animals and cattle, creeping things and flying birds,
leaders of the nations and all people,
kings, queens and rulers of the earth.
Let them all find their voice,
let them all hear the song,
for God created and we were made.

(from Psalms 146, 147)

(A time for reflection on the reading – silent or spoken)

Prayer

In the silence of our hearts or in spoken words
let us give thanks for the gift of this day
and pray for the life of the world . . .

(Here brief prayers may be offered)

Blessed are you, O God of justice.
Blessed are you, O God of beauty.
Blessed are you, O God of gentleness.
Blessed are you, O God of wild unbridled winds.
We find you in all things.
We find you in every creature.
We find you in the depths of our ever-living souls.
Praise be to you.

Closing Words

(after which candle is extinguished)

The blessings of heaven,
the blessings of earth,
the blessings of sea and of sky.
On those we love this day
and on every human family
the gifts of heaven,
the gifts of earth,
the gifts of sea and of sky.

BOOK SIX

The Good News of Jesus

DAY ONE
Opening Words
(as candle is lit)

We light a light
in the name of the God who creates life,
in the name of the Saviour who loves life,
in the name of the Spirit who is the fire of life.

*(Be still and aware of God's presence within
and all around)*

Scripture

In the beginning was the Word
and the Word was with God
and the Word was God.
He was in the beginning with God.
All things came into being through him
and without him not one thing came into being.
What has come into being in him was life
and the life was the light of all people.
The light shines in the darkness
and the darkness has not overcome it.
The Word was in the world,
and the world came into being through him,
yet the world did not know him.
So the Word became flesh and lived among us
and we have seen his glory,
like the glory of a newborn child,
full of grace and truth
From his fullness we have all received,
grace upon grace.
No one has ever seen God.
Jesus the Son has made the Eternal Mystery known.
He is close to the heart of God.
He has shown us the light that enlightens every person coming
   into the world.

(from John 1)

(A time for reflection on the reading – silent or spoken)

Prayer

In the silence of our hearts or in spoken words
let us give thanks for the gift of this day
and pray for the life of the world . . .

(Here brief prayers may be offered)

You have taught us, O Christ, to love the world.
You have shown us the light that is within us and
    within all things.
May we learn to love you more
and in loving you more
learn to love the earth and all its people more,
for you are the light of all life.

Closing Words
(after which candle is extinguished)

The blessings of heaven,
the blessings of earth,
the blessings of sea and of sky.
On those we love this day
and on every human family
the gifts of heaven,
the gifts of earth,
the gifts of sea and of sky.

DAY TWO
Opening Words
(as candle is lit)

We light a light
in the name of the God who creates life,
in the name of the Saviour who loves life,
in the name of the Spirit who is the fire of life.

*(Be still and aware of God's presence within
and all around)*

Scripture

There was a wedding in Cana of Galilee
and the mother of Jesus was there.
Jesus and his disciples had also been invited to the wedding.
The wine gave out halfway through the feast
and Jesus' mother said to him, 'They have no wine.'
Jesus said, 'But what concern is that to you and to me?
My time has not yet come.'
But his mother said to the servants, 'Do whatever he tells you.'
Standing nearby were six stone water-jars,
each holding twenty or thirty gallons.
Jesus said to the servants, 'Fill the jars with water.'
And they filled them up to the brim.
He said to them, 'Now draw some out and take it to the chief server.'
So they took it to the chief server
and when he tasted the water that had become wine
he called the bridegroom and said,
'Everyone serves the good wine first and then the cheaper wine
when the guests have become drunk.
But you have kept the good wine to the last.'
Jesus did this, the first of his signs, in Cana of Galilee.
And he revealed his glory and the disciples believed in him.

(from John 2)

(A time for reflection on the reading – silent or spoken)

Prayer

In the silence of our hearts or in spoken words
let us give thanks for the gift of this day
and pray for the life of the world . . .

(Here brief prayers may be offered)

You have shown us, O Christ, that grace changes life,
that grace can turn the ordinary into the festive
and emptiness into fullness.
When we find ourselves in you, O Christ,
we find that we too are bearers of grace
and that we too can be part of changing the world.

Closing Words
(after which candle is extinguished)

The blessings of heaven,
the blessings of earth,
the blessings of sea and of sky.
On those we love this day
and on every human family
the gifts of heaven,
the gifts of earth,
the gifts of sea and of sky.

DAY THREE
Opening Words
(as candle is lit)

We light a light
in the name of the God who creates life,
in the name of the Saviour who loves life,
in the name of the Spirit who is the fire of life.

*(Be still and aware of God's presence within
and all around)*

Scripture

After some time Jesus again came to Cana in Galilee
where he had changed the water into wine.
There was an officer of the king
whose young son lay ill in a nearby town.
When he heard that Jesus had come to Galilee
he went and begged him to heal his son
for he was very ill.
Jesus said, 'People do not believe unless they see signs and wonders.'
The royal officer said to him, 'Sir, come with me before
   my little boy dies.'
And Jesus replied, 'Go. Your son will live.'
The father believed what Jesus said and started on his way.
When he was halfway home his servants met him on the road
and they told him that his son was alive.
So he asked them at what hour the boy began to recover.
And they said to him, 'The fever left him yesterday at one
   in the afternoon.'
The father realized that this was the hour when Jesus had said,
'Your son will live.'
So he believed in Jesus
as did his whole household.
This was the second sign that Jesus did.
And he revealed his grace.

(from John 4)

(A time for reflection on the reading – silent or spoken)

Prayer

In the silence of our hearts or in spoken words
let us give thanks for the gift of this day
and pray for the life of the world . . .

(Here brief prayers may be offered)

You have shown us the way of compassion, O Christ.
You have shown us the heart of kindness.
Awaken the depths of compassion in us
that we may be alive to one another's suffering.
Awaken the heart of kindness in us
that we may be truly alive.

Closing Words
(after which candle is extinguished)

The blessings of heaven,
the blessings of earth,
the blessings of sea and of sky.
On those we love this day
and on every human family
the gifts of heaven,
the gifts of earth,
the gifts of sea and of sky.

DAY FOUR
Opening Words
(as candle is lit)

We light a light
in the name of the God who creates life,
in the name of the Saviour who loves life,
in the name of the Spirit who is the fire of life.

*(Be still and aware of God's presence within
and all around)*

Scripture

There was a man in Bethany who was very ill.
His name was Lazarus and his sisters were Mary and Martha.
They sent a message to Jesus, saying, 'The one whom you love is ill.'
So he said to his disciples, 'Our friend Lazarus has fallen asleep.
I am going to wake him up.'
After two days of travel Jesus approached Bethany
and learned that Lazarus had died.
When Martha heard that Jesus was coming she ran to meet him
    and said,
'Lord, if you had been here, my brother would not have died.'
And Jesus said to her, 'I am the resurrection and the life.
Those who believe in me, even though they die, will live'.
Martha ran back to the house to say to her sister,
'The Teacher is here and is calling for you.'
So Mary got up quickly and went to him
and when she found him she knelt at his feet with tears in her eyes
    and said,
'Lord, if you had been here, my brother would not have died.'
When Jesus saw her he wept.
And those who were present said, 'See how he loved him.'
They took Jesus to the tomb of Lazarus.
It was a cave with a stone laid against it.
And Jesus said, 'Take away the stone.'
But Martha objected: 'Lord, my brother has been dead four days.
Already there is a stench.'
Jesus said, 'Did I not tell you that if you believe you would see
    the glory of God?'

So they rolled the stone away.
And Jesus cried with a loud voice, 'Lazarus, come out!'
Lazarus stepped out of the cave, his body still bound in strips
of cloth.
Jesus said to them, 'Unbind him. Let him go.'
And there were many who believed because of this sign
but when word reached the religious leaders in Jerusalem
they were jealous.
And from that day they began to plot against Jesus.

(from John 11)

(A time for reflection on the reading – silent or spoken)

Prayer

In the silence of our hearts or in spoken words
let us give thanks for the gift of this day
and pray for the life of the world . . .

(Here brief prayers may be offered)

You wept at the death of a friend, O Christ,
you showed sorrow at the suffering of others.
Grant us the strength to express sadness
and the confidence to call forth new life.
Open our eyes to see every family as part of one family.
Open our lips to speak words of hope.

Closing Words

(after which candle is extinguished)

The blessings of heaven,
the blessings of earth,
the blessings of sea and of sky.
On those we love this day
and on every human family
the gifts of heaven,
the gifts of earth,
the gifts of sea and of sky.

DAY FIVE
Opening Words
(as candle is lit)

We light a light
in the name of the God who creates life,
in the name of the Saviour who loves life,
in the name of the Spirit who is the fire of life.

*(Be still and aware of God's presence within
and all around)*

Scripture

Jesus entered Jerusalem during the festival of Passover
and when the people heard that he was coming
they went out to greet him with palm branches and song.
'Hosanna!' they cried. 'Blessed is he who comes in the name of God.'
Jesus rode into the heart of the city on a young donkey.
And people remembered what was written in the scriptures,
'Do not be afraid, O daughters of Jerusalem.
Look, your king is coming, riding on a colt.'
The religious leaders felt threatened by him and plotted his arrest.
On the evening of Passover Jesus met with his disciples in the city.
During the meal he got up from the table, took off his outer robe,
tied a towel around himself and poured water into a basin.
He began to wash the disciples' feet and to dry them with the towel.
When he was finished he returned to the table and said,
'Do you know what I have done to you?
You call me Master and Teacher, and you are right for that is what I am.
So if I your Master and Teacher have washed your feet
you also should wash one another's feet.
I have set you an example, that you should do as I have done to you.
I give you a new commandment, that you should love one another.
As I have loved you so love one another.
By this everyone will know that you are my followers.'
After the meal Jesus withdrew with his disciples to a garden.
But Judas, who was to betray him, also knew the garden
for it was a place where Jesus often met with his disciples.

(from John 12–13)

(A time for reflection on the reading – silent or spoken)

Prayer

In the silence of our hearts or in spoken words
let us give thanks for the gift of this day
and pray for the life of the world . . .

(Here brief prayers may be offered)

You knew betrayal in your life, O Christ.
One whom you loved turned against you.
Our lives are filled with betrayals.
Men and women and whole communities turn
   against one another.
Strengthen us in the way of faithfulness, O Christ,
that we may be true to you, to our own depths and
   to one another.
Strengthen us in the way of faithfulness.

Closing Words
(after which candle is extinguished)

The blessings of heaven,
the blessings of earth,
the blessings of sea and of sky.
On those we love this day
and on every human family
the gifts of heaven,
the gifts of earth,
the gifts of sea and of sky.

DAY SIX
Opening Words
(as candle is lit)

We light a light
in the name of the God who creates life,
in the name of the Saviour who loves life,
in the name of the Spirit who is the fire of life.

*(Be still and aware of God's presence within
and all around)*

Scripture

The disciple Judas betrayed his Master.
He led soldiers to the garden where Jesus was praying
and there they arrested him.
They took him to the chief priest's house
and from there to the headquarters of the Roman government.
Pilate the Governor asked Jesus, 'Are you a king as people say you are?'
Jesus answered, 'I came into the world to reveal the truth.
And everyone who belongs to the kingdom of truth listens
    to my voice.'
Pilate was worried by these words but handed Jesus over to be beaten.
The soldiers wove a crown of thorns for his head and hit him
    in the face.
They dressed him in purple like a king and mocked him.
Then Pilate brought Jesus back to the chief priests and said,
'I find no case against this man. Let him go.'
But they shouted, 'Crucify him! Crucify him!
He should die, for he claims to be the Son of God.'
When Pilate heard this he was even more worried and asked Jesus,
'Where are you from? Why will you not answer me?
Do you not know that I have the power to let you go or the power
    to kill you?'
And Jesus said, 'You would have no power unless it was given
    from above.'
Then Pilate handed Jesus over to be crucified.
They took him and forced him to carry his cross through the city.
And on a hill called Golgotha they crucified him with a criminal
    on either side.

Standing near the cross were women who had followed him to
    Jerusalem,
Jesus' mother, his mother's sister, Mary Magdalene and others.
And when Jesus saw the disciple whom he loved standing beside
    his mother
he said, 'Mother, here is your son.'
And to the disciple, he said, 'And here is your mother.'
From that hour the disciple took Jesus' mother into his own home.
But Jesus, broken by his sufferings on the cross, said, 'It is finished.'
And he bowed his head and breathed his last.
Jesus the Son of Glory was dead.

(from John 18–19)

(A time for reflection on the reading – silent or spoken)

Prayer

In the silence of our hearts or in spoken words
let us give thanks for the gift of this day
and pray for the life of the world . . .

(Here brief prayers may be offered)

At the very last, O Christ,
you remembered your mother and the disciple you loved.
Show us the way of love.
Teach us to remember one another.
And reassure us that it is when we give ourselves away in love
that we truly find ourselves.
Show us the way of love, O Christ.

Closing Words
(after which candle is extinguished)

The blessings of heaven,
the blessings of earth,
the blessings of sea and of sky.
On those we love this day
and on every human family
the gifts of heaven,
the gifts of earth,
the gifts of sea and of sky.

DAY SEVEN
Opening Words
(as candle is lit)

We light a light
in the name of the God who creates life,
in the name of the Saviour who loves life,
in the name of the Spirit who is the fire of life.

*(Be still and aware of God's presence within
and all around)*

Scripture

There was a garden in the place where Jesus was crucified
and in the garden was a tomb in which Jesus' body was laid.
He was wrapped in linen cloths with a precious mixture of myrrh
  and spices.
Early on the first day of the week, while it was still very dark,
Mary Magdalene came to the garden.
She saw that the stone had been rolled away from the tomb.
So she ran to tell Peter and the disciple whom Jesus loved.
'They have taken the Master from the tomb,' she said,
'and I do not know where they have laid him.'
Then the two disciples hurried to the garden and found the tomb
  empty,
apart from the linen cloths that had been used to wrap Jesus' body.
Mary remained in the garden after the disciples had gone.
She stood weeping outside the tomb.
But as she wept she looked into the tomb and saw two angels of light.
They were sitting where the body of Jesus had been laid,
one at the head and the other at the foot.
Then she turned around and saw him but she did not know
  that it was Jesus.
He said to her, 'Woman, why are you weeping? And who are you
  looking for?'
Supposing him to be the gardener, Mary said,
'Sir, if you have carried the body away please tell me where you have
  laid him.'
Jesus said to her, 'Mary!'
And she recognized his voice and said, 'Teacher!'

'Do not try to hold me,' said Jesus, 'for I am returning to God.
Tell the disciples what you have seen and say to them,
"I am going to my Father and your Father, to my God and your God." '
So Mary Magdalene went and said to the disciples, 'I have seen
   the Lord.'
This was the first sign that Jesus did after his death.
And he revealed his presence to them.
There are many other things that could be told about Jesus
but if every one of them were reported
I suppose the world itself could not contain the books that would
   be written.

(from John 20)

(A time for reflection on the reading – silent or spoken)

Prayer

In the silence of our hearts or in spoken words
let us give thanks for the gift of this day
and pray for the life of the world . . .

(Here brief prayers may be offered)

O Christ who died yet lives
and who is among us as one who has returned to God,
your words speak to us from the centre of our hearts,
you address us from the garden of our souls.
Call us by name that we may recognize you within us and among us.
Show us your wounds that in the brokenness of life
we may glimpse your resurrection presence.

Closing Words

(after which candle is extinguished)

The blessings of heaven,
the blessings of earth,
the blessings of sea and of sky.
On those we love this day
and on every human family
the gifts of heaven,
the gifts of earth,
the gifts of sea and of sky.

BOOK SEVEN

Letters of Love

DAY ONE

Opening Words
(as candle is lit)

We light a light
in the name of the God who creates life,
in the name of the Saviour who loves life,
in the name of the Spirit who is the fire of life.

*(Be still and aware of God's presence within
and all around)*

Scripture

Grace to you and peace from God, who was and is and is to come,
and from Jesus Christ the faithful one,
the firstborn of the dead and prince of all creation.
I, John, a follower of Christ was imprisoned on the island of Patmos.
On the first day of the week I was in prayer and heard behind me a voice.
So I turned to see whose voice it was that spoke to me
and when I turned I saw seven golden lampstands.
In the middle of the lamps I saw one who looked like the Son of Humanity.
He was clothed in a long robe with a golden sash across his chest.
His hair was as white as snow and his eyes were like a flame of fire.
His face was like the midday sun blazing with full force.
His feet were glistening like bronze
and his voice was like the sound of many waters.
In his right hand he held seven stars
and from his mouth came a sharp two-edged sword.
When I saw him I fell at his feet with fear.
But he placed his hand on me and said, 'Do not be afraid.
I am the first and the last and the living one.
I was dead, and see, I am alive forever.
And I have the keys of death and hell.
As for the mystery of the seven stars that you saw in my right hand
they are the angels of the seven churches.
And the seven lampstands among which you saw me walking,
they are the seven churches.
Let anyone who has an ear listen to what the Spirit is saying.'

(from Revelation 1)

(A time for reflection on the reading – silent or spoken)

Prayer

In the silence of our hearts or in spoken words
let us give thanks for the gift of this day
and pray for the life of the world . . .

(Here brief prayers may be offered)

You are within us and among us, O Christ,
as the one who is alive for ever.
In the sorrows and sufferings of our lives you are with us
as the one who holds the keys of new beginnings.
There is no ending in the world,
there is no fear in our lives,
there is no despair in our hearts,
that your living presence cannot unlock.
You are within us and among us, O Christ,
as the one who is alive for ever.

Closing Words
(after which candle is extinguished)

The blessings of heaven,
the blessings of earth,
the blessings of sea and of sky.
On those we love this day
and on every human family
the gifts of heaven,
the gifts of earth,
the gifts of sea and of sky.

DAY TWO
Opening Words
(as candle is lit)

We light a light
in the name of the God who creates life,
in the name of the Saviour who loves life,
in the name of the Spirit who is the fire of life.

*(Be still and aware of God's presence within
and all around)*

Scripture

This is the message we have heard from the beginning,
that we should love one another.
Whoever does not love is not truly alive.
We know that we have passed from death to life if we love.
This is why Jesus came, to make us truly alive.
So let us love, not only in word and speech, but in truth and action.
By this we know that we are of the truth.
By this we can be sure within ourselves,
even when our hearts condemn us.
So, beloved, let us love one another, for love is of God.
Everyone who loves is born of God and knows God.
And whoever does not love does not know God, for God is love.
Love was shown to us in Jesus.
He laid down his life for us.
And we should lay down our lives for one another.
No one has ever seen God,
but, if we love one another, God lives in us.
God is love,
and those who live in love live in God and God lives in them.
There is no fear in love,
for perfect love casts out fear.
This is the message we have heard from the beginning,
that those who love God should also love one another.

(from 1 John 3–4)

(A time for reflection on the reading – silent or spoken)

Prayer

In the silence of our hearts or in spoken words
let us give thanks for the gift of this day
and pray for the life of the world . . .

(Here brief prayers may be offered)

You have shown us love, O Christ.
You have shown us God.
Show us also our true face
and the true face of every human being.
Show us the desire for love and the strength to give
   ourselves in love
that are woven into the fabric of our being.
For we are made in the image of love, O Christ.
We are made in the image of God.

Closing Words
(after which candle is extinguished)

The blessings of heaven,
the blessings of earth,
the blessings of sea and of sky.
On those we love this day
and on every human family
the gifts of heaven,
the gifts of earth,
the gifts of sea and of sky.

DAY THREE

Opening Words

(as candle is lit)

We light a light
in the name of the God who creates life,
in the name of the Saviour who loves life,
in the name of the Spirit who is the fire of life.

*(Be still and aware of God's presence within
and all around)*

Scripture

James, the brother of Jesus and servant of God, to those living in exile:
Brothers and sisters,
welcome with humility the word of God that has been planted within you.
It has the power to save your souls.
Every generous act of giving, like every perfect gift, is from above.
It comes from the Giver of lights
in whom there is no shadow of falseness.
Understand this, my dear ones,
let everyone be quick to listen,
slow to speak and slow in anger,
for anger does not lead to right relationships.
Be doers of the word and not merely hearers.
For the golden rule of scripture is, 'Love your neighbour as yourself.'
What good is it, beloved,
if you say you have faith but do not have works?
Can faith alone save you?
If a brother or sister is naked and lacks daily food
and one of you says to them, 'Go in peace, keep warm and eat well',
what good will that do if you do not also help them practically?
So faith by itself, if it has no works, is dead.
Faith without action is barren.
Just as the body without the spirit is dead
so faith without works is dead.

(from James 1–2)

(A time for reflection on the reading – silent or spoken)

Prayer

In the silence of our hearts or in spoken words
let us give thanks for the gift of this day
and pray for the life of the world . . .

(Here brief prayers may be offered)

You have taught us, O Christ, to love our neighbour as our self.
You have taught us to see our neighbour as part of our self.
Let us see ourselves in those who are hungry.
Let us see ourselves in those who are frightened.
Let us see ourselves in one another and in every creature.
For you have taught us, O Christ, that we are one body.

Closing Words
(after which candle is extinguished)

The blessings of heaven,
the blessings of earth,
the blessings of sea and of sky.
On those we love this day
and on every human family
the gifts of heaven,
the gifts of earth,
the gifts of sea and of sky.

DAY FOUR
Opening Words
(as candle is lit)

We light a light
in the name of the God who creates life,
in the name of the Saviour who loves life,
in the name of the Spirit who is the fire of life.

*(Be still and aware of God's presence within
and all around)*

Scripture

Peter, a follower of Christ, to those living in exile:
May grace and peace be yours in abundance.
And may you live in a spirit of unity together,
with sympathy, love, tender hearts and humble minds.
Do not repay evil for evil or abuse for abuse.
Instead repay wrong with acts of grace.
As the scriptures say,
'Turn away from evil and do good.
Seek peace and pursue it.
For the eyes of God are on those who seek right relationships.
And the face of God is against those who do wrong.'
Even if you suffer for doing right, you are blessed,
for that is what Christ did in bringing us to God.
He was put to death in the flesh but made alive in the spirit.
So if Christ suffered physically
we also should be prepared to suffer.
Be strong in your love for one another.
Be generous without complaining.
Serve one another with the gifts you have been given.
And when you speak let your words be words of love.
In this way God will be honoured in everything you do.

(from 1 Peter 3–4)

(A time for reflection on the reading silent or spoken)

Prayer

In the silence of our hearts or in spoken words
let us give thanks for the gift of this day
and pray for the life of the world . . .

(Here brief prayers may be offered)

O Christ, who died in the flesh but was made alive in the spirit
and who suffered hatred in showing us love,
let us find our deepest longings in you,
the desire for peace that is deeper than strife,
the yearning for unity that is deeper than division.
Set free these longings in our hearts, O Christ.
Set free the true longings of our hearts.

Closing Words
(after which candle is extinguished)

The blessings of heaven,
the blessings of earth,
the blessings of sea and of sky.
On those we love this day
and on every human family
the gifts of heaven,
the gifts of earth,
the gifts of sea and of sky.

DAY FIVE
Opening Words
(as candle is lit)

We light a light
in the name of the God who creates life,
in the name of the Saviour who loves life,
in the name of the Spirit who is the fire of life.

*(Be still and aware of God's presence within
and all around)*

Scripture

Paul, a follower of Christ, to the church in Corinth:
Grace to you and peace from God.
We are one body in Christ
and by one Spirit we all have been baptized,
whether Jew or Greek, male or female, slave or free.
If one member of the body suffers, all suffer together,
and if one member is honoured, all are honoured.
This is the way of love.
If I speak with the tongues of angels but do not have love
I am a noisy gong or a clanging cymbal.
If I have prophetic powers and understand all mysteries and
   all knowledge,
and if I have faith to remove mountains,
but do not have love, I am nothing.
If I give away all my possessions and sacrifice my life
but do not have love, I gain nothing.
Love is patient. Love is kind.
Love is not jealous or boastful or proud or rude.
It does not insist on its own way.
It is not bad-tempered or resentful.
It does not delight in wrong but rejoices in what is right.
It bears all things, believes all things,
hopes all things, endures all things.
Love never ends.

(from 1 Corinthians 12–13)

(A time for reflection on the reading – silent or spoken)

Prayer

In the silence of our hearts or in spoken words
let us give thanks for the gift of this day
and pray for the life of the world . . .

(Here brief prayers may be offered)

In you, O Christ, we find that we are one,
whether east or west,
whether parent or child,
whether human or creature.
Renew us in life's unity.
Release in us again the mighty flow of the one river.
And set us free, O Christ, to love.

Closing Words

(after which candle is extinguished)

The blessings of heaven,
the blessings of earth,
the blessings of sea and of sky.
On those we love this day
and on every human family
the gifts of heaven,
the gifts of earth,
the gifts of sea and of sky.

DAY SIX
Opening Words
(as candle is lit)

We light a light
in the name of the God who creates life,
in the name of the Saviour who loves life,
in the name of the Spirit who is the fire of life.

*(Be still and aware of God's presence within
and all around)*

Scripture

Paul, a prisoner for Christ, to the church in Ephesus:
Grace to you and peace from God.
You have probably heard how God's grace was given to me
and how the mystery of Christ was made known to me.
I have become a servant of the Gospel
to share the news of the boundless riches of Christ
and to bring to light the plan of the mystery hidden for ages in God
who created all things.
The treasure of God's wisdom is now being made known to all people.
For this reason I bow my knee before the Giver of life
from whom every family in heaven and on earth takes its name.
I pray that you may be strengthened in your inner being
through the power of the Spirit
and that Christ may be present in your hearts through faith
as you are rooted and grounded in love.
I also pray that you may come to know
what is the breadth and length and height and depth
and to experience the love of Christ that is greater than all knowledge
so that you may be filled with the fullness of God.
Now to the One who by the power at work within us
is able to do far more than we could ever ask or imagine,
to God be glory for ever and ever.

(from Ephesians 3)

(A time for reflection on the reading – silent or spoken)

Prayer

In the silence of our hearts or in spoken words
let us give thanks for the gift of this day
and pray for the life of the world . . .

(Here brief prayers may be offered)

O Christ, in whom the fullness of God dwells,
you are deep within our lives and all life,
you are deep within this place and every place.
In this place and this time and in the depths of our own souls
we draw from the inner well of your love
that we too might be filled with the fullness of God
and that you might do within us and in our world
far more than we could ever ask or imagine.

Closing Words
(after which candle is extinguished)

The blessings of heaven,
the blessings of earth,
the blessings of sea and of sky.
On those we love this day
and on every human family
the gifts of heaven,
the gifts of earth,
the gifts of sea and of sky.

DAY SEVEN
Opening Words
(as candle is lit)

We light a light
in the name of the God who creates life,
in the name of the Saviour who loves life,
in the name of the Spirit who is the fire of life.

*(Be still and aware of God's presence within
and all around)*

Scripture

Faith is the assurance of things hoped for,
the conviction of things not yet seen.
By faith our ancestors received confidence.
By faith we understand that the world was made by
  the word of God
so that what is seen was born from what is not seen.
By faith Abraham and Sarah obeyed God
when they set out from their homeland
not knowing where the journey would take them.
By faith they received the birth of a child
when Abraham was frail and Sarah was barren.
Thus from an old couple generations of children were born,
as many as the stars of heaven.
Abraham and Sarah died believing
but they did not receive everything that had been promised.
It was from a distance that they saw and greeted the future.
By faith Moses was hidden by his mother for three months
  after his birth
because she saw that her child was beautiful
and had the courage to disobey Pharaoh.
By faith the Hebrew slaves followed Moses and Miriam through
  the Sea of Reeds
as if it were dry land, and the chariots of Egypt were destroyed.
What more should I say?
Time itself would fail me to tell of David or Judith,
Rebekah or Ezekiel, or the many others who died believing.
All of these, though they are remembered for their faith,

did not receive everything that was promised.
God had something better planned that was still to come.
Therefore since we are surrounded by so great a cloud of witnesses
let us also put aside every weight and sin that distracts us
and run the race that is ahead of us,
looking to Jesus the leader and perfecter of our faith,
who for the sake of love endured the road of suffering
and has gone ahead of us into the heart of God.

(from Hebrews 11–12)

(A time for reflection on the reading – silent or spoken)

Prayer

In the silence of our hearts or in spoken words
let us give thanks for the gift of this day
and pray for the life of the world . . .

(Here brief prayers may be offered)

O Christ, who is the leader of our faith,
show us the Way.
O Christ, who suffered for the sake of love,
show us the Truth.
O Christ, who has gone ahead of us into the heart of God,
show us the Life,
the Life that creates life,
the Life that saves life,
the Life that loves life.

Closing Words
(after which candle is extinguished)

The blessings of heaven,
the blessings of earth,
the blessings of sea and of sky.
On those we love this day
and on every human family
the gifts of heaven,
the gifts of earth,
the gifts of sea and of sky.

APPENDIX

Celtic Art Illustrations

The ancient Celtic art used throughout this publication is from *The Book of Kells*, an illuminated Gospel manuscript over 1,200 years old. It consists of nearly 700 pages of Gospel text, some of which is elaborately decorated, and was produced in the Columban monastic tradition, probably on the holy island of Iona off the west coast of Scotland. In its early history it was simply referred to as The Gospel of Columcille (or Columba), the great missionary saint whose monastic communities had spread from Ireland to Scotland and England in the sixth and seventh centuries. By the early ninth century, however, repeated Scandinavian raids on the monastic libraries and treasures of Iona led the Columban community to establish its motherhouse in the relative safety of Kells in County Meath, Ireland. Thus the manuscript came to be called *The Book of Kells*, even though it is unlikely that any of the artwork or transcription occurred there. Since the seventeenth century it has been housed in the Library of Trinity College, Dublin.

While *The Book of Kells* is the most spectacular illuminated manuscript from this period in Ireland and Britain, its themes are typical of the ancient Celtic Christian tradition. The artwork speaks of a vision of all things interrelated, both seen and unseen, creaturely and human, and heaven and earth. The interlacing patterns, so characteristic of the Kells manuscript, weave together the whole of reality. Nothing is omitted. Plants and animals, angelic faces and human forms, birds, fish and creatures of the deep, many of which are purely imaginary shapes and sizes, appear not only in the highly decorated opening pages of the four Gospels but also in between the lines of Gospel text itself. And often there is no apparent reason for a cat, a mouse, a dragon or a hen to suddenly appear amid texts communicating the mysteries of Christ's birth, death and resurrection, other than to make the point again and again that the natural and the sacred are inseparably interwoven, and that the thread that connects God's life with all life can be discerned everywhere. There is a twin-love of Christ and Creation in the Celtic tradition. Never are they far apart.

Little is known of the scribes and artists who worked in the scriptoria of the ancient Columban monastic communities to produce these magical works. We do not know how many hands were involved in the creative genius of *The Book of Kells*, although art historians have noted at least three significant styles. One has been called 'the Goldsmith' because of the metalwork effect that is achieved, for example, on the Chi-Rho page, on the front cover of this book (Chi and Rho being the first two letters of Christ's name in Greek). Another has been designated 'the Illustrator' because of his expertise in depicting Gospel scenes such as the temptation and the arrest of Christ. And the third has been called 'the Portrait Painter' because of his compositions of Christ and the Evangelists. All three of these artists, and there may well have been more, were painting with colours derived from mineral and plant pigments from all over the then known world, lapis-lazuli, for instance, probably being supplied from as far away as Afghanistan.

This is a striking feature of the artwork of *The Book of Kells* and related illuminated manuscripts of the period. The Columban monastic communities may have been working in what today seem like isolated islands along the Atlantic coastline of Ireland and Britain, but clearly there was a sense of connection between east and west that was fostered by ancient trade routes and the exchange of divergent ideas and art forms. The art of the Celtic world bears extraordinary similarities to the ancient art of Egypt and the Coptic Christian world of the earliest centuries. This is part of the resurgent appeal of Celtic imagery today. It reflects a way of seeing that is broader than our classical Greek and Roman inheritance. It reintroduces us to forgotten treasure.